Leveraging Today's Social Media

Leveraging Today's Social Media
Its Role in School District Improvement and Success

MARK D. BENIGNI
BARBARA A. HAEFFNER
SUSAN O. MOORE
JEFFREY F. SOLAN

BLOOMSBURY ACADEMIC
NEW YORK · LONDON · OXFORD · NEW DELHI · SYDNEY

BLOOMSBURY ACADEMIC

Bloomsbury Publishing Inc, 1359 Broadway, New York, NY 10018, USA
Bloomsbury Publishing Plc, 50 Bedford Square, London, WC1B 3DP, UK
Bloomsbury Publishing Ireland, 29 Earlsfort Terrace, Dublin 2, D02 AY28, Ireland

BLOOMSBURY, BLOOMSBURY ACADEMIC and the Diana logo are trademarks of Bloomsbury Publishing Plc

First published in the United States of America 2026

Copyright © Mark D. Benigni, Barbara A. Haeffner, Susan O. Moore, Jeffrey F. Solan 2026

For legal purposes the Acknowledgments on p. xvii constitute an extension of this copyright page.

Cover design: Chloe Batch
Cover image © iStock.com/master1305

All rights reserved. No part of this publication may be: i) reproduced or transmitted in any form, electronic or mechanical, including photocopying, recording or by means of any information storage or retrieval system without prior permission in writing from the publishers; or ii) used or reproduced in any way for the training, development or operation of artificial intelligence (AI) technologies, including generative AI technologies. The rights holders expressly reserve this publication from the text and data mining exception as per Article 4(3) of the Digital Single Market Directive (EU) 2019/790.

Bloomsbury Publishing Inc does not have any control over, or responsibility for, any third-party websites referred to or in this book. All internet addresses given in this book were correct at the time of going to press. The author and publisher regret any inconvenience caused if addresses have changed or sites have ceased to exist, but can accept no responsibility for any such changes.

A catalog record for this book is available from the Library of Congress.

ISBN: HB: 978-1-4758-7288-0
PB: 978-1-4758-7289-7
ePDF: 979-8-2163-8314-7
eBook: 978-1-4758-7290-3

Typeset by Deanta Global Publishing Services, Chennai, India
Printed and bound in the United States of America

For product safety related questions contact productsafety@bloomsbury.com.

To find out more about our authors and books visit www.bloomsbury.com and sign up for our newsletters.

To the students who teach, challenge, and inspire us every day and to Lois Lehman, our mentor and friend, who makes us better educators.

I would like to dedicate this book to the Meriden community and all my past teachers and professors who taught me what type of educator and leader I wanted to be. It was our interactions together that defined me as a teacher, school administrator, and district leader. A special thank you to my mom, Gail, my late father, Jack, and Laura for providing me so much love and support. Lastly, to my children, Bria and Blake, who are emerging young adults. You have given my life passion and purpose, and I am so proud of you!
— Mark Benigni

Dedicated to my parents, Bob and Shirley, whose unwavering support has inspired me. I am also grateful to my husband, Scott, for his love and constant encouragement.
—Barbara Haeffner

This book is dedicated to educators—past, present, and future—who share ideas, challenges, and best practices to help us all improve for the benefit of our students, staff, and families. I am also grateful to my husband, Tom, and my children, Katie and Johnathon, for their unwavering love and support.
—Susan Moore

This book is dedicated to the incredible teachers, students, staff, board members, families, and community members that comprise the Cheshire Public Schools. The love and gratitude for my wife, Dara, and sons, Avery and Grayson, is boundless. Thank you for the joy you bring and your understanding and support as I try to be the best professional I can be.
—*Jeffrey Solan*

Contents

Foreword viii
Preface xv
Acknowledgments xvii

1   **#GoingSocial: Introduction** 1

2   **#HiringSocial: Talent Management and Professional Learning** 23

3   **#LearningSocial: Curriculum and Instruction** 39

4   **#CelebratingSocial: Building a Positive Climate and Culture** 59

5   **#LeveragingSocial: Systems and Operations** 75

6   **#LeadingSocial: Making Connections** 89

In Closing 101

Moving Forward 103
References 108
About the Authors 110

Foreword

"I use social media both for teaching and for my personal life; that's the real reality that we want to prepare our students for because they're not going to step into a world where they have to surrender their cell phone devices. They need to be prepared to navigate a world where they can discern between the positive ways of using networking and social networking versus the negative."

—Connecticut High School Teacher

"Social media is being used right? We all know that. And that's the kids' number one go-to ... kids use social media. So let's get them educated. It's not going away. We're not going to sweep it under the rug. They're not putting away their cell phones."

—Connecticut Middle School Counselor

"We learned a lot, my husband and I, when we joined social media platforms with our kids, we learned a lot about digital etiquette [and that] was huge. We learned a lot about how our kids function on a social media platform. And do we understand it with minutiae? Not even close. But being willing to engage in social media with our children, even if it's an invasive space, I know some kids are like, "Oh, well, I don't even want my parent in the same room as me, let alone in my social media platform. I think it behooves a lot of parents to be there with them, [it] would be a huge education about who their kids are when they're not around, people that they're becoming. I think it would be wise for a lot of parents to make the effort to engage and see what that looks like."

—Connecticut High School Parent

These sentiments were shared by participants from our *Social Media and Mental Health Study*. We interviewed over seventy parents, teachers, counselors, and administrators across four school districts in Connecticut during the 2023–4 school year to understand how they perceived the effects of social media on adolescents' lives. Participants in our study expressed their concerns about how social media affects student learning and mental health, promotes misinformation and problematic social comparisons, reduces attention spans, exposes users to risks, alters children's abilities to form in-person relationships, and leads to other concerning outcomes.

Simultaneously, the majority of those we spoke to accepted that for most children, and adults for that matter, social media is a lifeline that permeates all corners of life and may lead to positive outcomes. For example, some participants expressed how social media allows children to form and maintain meaningful relationships with others across great distances. Others talked about how they observed young people discover passions and interests, and find supportive communities online. Our participants, primarily self-identified Gen Xers or Millennials who did not grow up as digital natives like Gen Z or Gen Alpha, actively attempted to reconcile their recognition of these positive effects of social media with their desire to protect youth from its risks. They were eager to understand how to better support themselves and their students or children in navigating digital media in a more healthy way.

These findings align with the broader public narrative that social media and personal technology use harms children. The strength of this public narrative, particularly that social media is associated with, and even perhaps causes mental health issues for adolescents (Twenge et al., 2018), echoed loudly throughout our conversations. This message has been bolstered by the recent release of Jonathan Haidt's book *The Anxious Generation: How the Great Rewiring of Childhood Is Causing an Epidemic of Mental Illness*, which became an almost instant phenomenon. When others find out that we research social media use and adolescent mental health, whether it be at social gatherings, our children's sports games, or at professional conferences, they ask us if we have read this book. They often follow up with questions about whether they should ban or restrict social media and related technology from their children's lives. In response, we often give what they may perceive as a somewhat unsatisfactory, but honest answer beginning with, "It depends." Along with many other researchers, we remain cautious of deficit-framed narratives depicting social media as entirely problematic without nuanced consideration and investigation into how it is used, by whom, and under what conditions (Moreno & Radesky, 2023; Odgers & Jensen, 2020).

We are researchers, but we are also educators, caregivers, parents, and fellow denizens; we can relate to feeling uncertain about how rapidly evolving technology affects us, our loved ones, and our students. However, existing research reflects the double-edged sword theme that our participants discussed—social media use can have both positive and negative effects on adolescents (American Psychological Association [APA], 2023). Problematic use of social media can indeed lead to negative social comparison, cyberbullying, and misinformation, which can contribute to mental health issues such as anxiety and depression. However, students can also positively engage in social media in ways that lead to identity development, self-exploration, and connection, which contribute to positive well-being (APA, 2023; Seabrook et al., 2016). Thus far, many of the interventions addressing surrounding social media use have been grounded in measuring and monitoring "screen time" to improve mental health outcomes (Riehm et al., 2019; Twenge et al., 2018). However, research on "screen time" does not investigate *how* students are using digital media. Simply reducing digital media use to "screen time" may be insufficient in empowering students to make better digital decisions across multiple domains of their lives for longer-term positive effects (Nesi et al., 2020). Are students passively scrolling through social media on their phones or other devices, or are they actively engaged in conversing with friends?

The narrative of social media and its effects is not as simple as conveyed in the public narrative. Disentangling the complex relationship between social media use and adolescent mental health is critical to enhancing efforts that support adolescent students. It requires a more nuanced approach to building students' agency to make decisions that lead to healthier digital habits (Moreno & Radesky, 2023), as solely removing phones from schools, without educating students on how to use these devices in the hours they are not in school, may not address our participants' or the public's perceived concerns.

As the authors of this book underscore, digital media—inclusive of social media—is here to stay. Over the past ten years, the percentage of Americans owning a smartphone has increased from 53 percent to 91 percent. Approximately 95 percent of teens report having access to a smartphone (Anderson et al., 2023). Adolescents use personal cell phones to access social media, the Internet, games, learning applications, and communication platforms in almost all environments—school, home, work, sports, clubs, after-school programs, and community organizations. Without digital media, many may miss out on essential opportunities to build relationships, learn, share, develop professionally, engage in a global world, gather information, and discover interests. It is an essential educational tool. Rather than shying away from technology, we should be embracing it.

Yet, in the United States, a growing number of state laws and policies that require, recommend, or incentivize the restriction of cell phone use in schools have been implemented this past year. Four states incentivize the implementation of school policies that restrict cell phone use. Five others require the development and adoption of school policies that restrict cell phone use. At the most restrictive level, three states outright ban cell phone use in schools. Connecticut is one of seven states that recommends school districts adopt a policy regarding restrictions or removal of cell phones in schools (Prothero et al., 2024). Following these trends, we anticipate that more states will adopt similar restrictive school cell phone policies in the coming months and years. However, little research context has demonstrated that cell phone bans in schools have long-lasting effects on students' learning and well-being, and these studies often come from outside the United States (e.g., Abrahamsson, 2024). Though these bans align with the concerns reflected in the public narrative, the scholarship does not conclusively support these actions.

The guidance accompanying these bans often fails to account for the fact that we need to educate children, parents, educators, and other constituents about how to navigate digital media and act as good digital citizens (Weinstein & James, 2022). It is akin to giving someone the keys to a car without any education or training, and expecting them to drive alone without any issues or accidents. Asset-based approaches supported by the authors of this book provide inroads for these educational opportunities and allow us to level digital media more broadly for learning and success.

We are at a critical inflection point in the development of our narrative and action around digital media use for adolescents. As these restrictive school cell phone laws and policies grow across our country, we ask ourselves, to what end? What are their purposes? Will removing cell phones from schools change students' long-term digital media habits? What is our shared responsibility to ensure adolescents are prepared to engage healthily in a digital world, outside of school and into their adulthood? To what degree do we need to shift our mindsets, practices, and policies to address digital agency, citizenship, and agency in our schools? How can we prepare students, parents, teachers, counselors, and administrators to embrace digital media in today's society while protecting them from its potential ills? What would happen if we reframed the current narrative around social media use from preventing negative effects to proactively promoting healthy use? What would it mean to embrace the possibility of technology in schools? How can social media be used as a tool for school district improvement and success?

We invite you, the reader, to consider these questions with an open mind as you read this book, *Leveraging Today's Social Media: Its Role in School District Improvement and Success*. The authors include Meriden Public Schools' Superintendent Dr. Mark D. Benigni, Assistant Superintendent of Teaching and Innovation Barbara A. Haeffner, Director of Instructional Technology and Curriculum Susan O. Moore, and Cheshire Public Schools' Superintendent Dr. Jeffrey F. Solan. These Connecticut-based educators have extensive expertise in teaching, school leadership, and educational innovation. Dr. Benigni is a transformative leader who is recognized for his innovation and success in urban education. Dr. Solan has led Cheshire Public Schools into an era of expansion and record-setting academic achievement in the state of Connecticut.

As dedicated educators, they have experienced the same confusion and worry about how to address social media and other technology, yet they have found ways to leverage technology to enhance the educational experience of students, families, and staff. They acknowledge the real concerns that our teachers, parents, counselors, and community members have regarding social media use while offering a needed fresh, practitioner-based perspective that reframes our conversations around this topic from being entrenched in fear to imbued with optimism. Drawing on real-world examples from their collective experience as district leaders, they provide concrete recommendations for how to use social media to better school systems in service to students. Each chapter focuses on pragmatic ways to embrace digital media and technology across multiple domains such as hiring, learning, culture building, enhancing school operations, increasing community engagement, and leading. Chapter 1 identifies the challenges and opportunities of using social media within a school district, how districts can determine how to use social media, and how social media can support school improvement efforts, among other topics. In Chapter 2, the authors describe how social media can be used in talent management and professional development related to staff, notably teachers. We often forget that many teachers, particularly new hires, are digital natives, and social media may serve as an effective means to support the learning and development of these professionals. Chapter 3 addresses how social media and other technologies like artificial intelligence can be leveraged in the curriculum and by educators in their instruction. In Chapter 4, the authors explore how social media and other technology can be used to build community and improve the climate within schools across constituents. Chapter 5 explores how district leaders can use social media and other technology to improve district systems and operations. In Chapter 6, the authors conclude with ten concrete lessons to guide school districts in the United States in beginning and maintaining campaigns that both recognize the challenges associated with social media and harness its power for school improvement in the digital age.

    This book is essential to our work as educators and educational leaders right now. Like the authors, many of us did not grow up with smartphones or social media. However, the world has changed and will continue to advance with the advent of new applications and innovations. The authors call us to consider how we can keep up with this evolution and support students and school communities in developing citizenship to embrace the possibilities of technology. Of course, this responsibility does not fall squarely on our shoulders. Addressing social media and technology use and mental health in schools requires an integrated, multipronged approach. It relies on prioritizing this issue at the federal, state, district, school, family, and community levels and allocating appropriate resources to this topic. However, as the authors remind us, we can drive a change in how we speak about digital media and how we educate our community about its potential positive and negative effects.

Our research underscores what the authors of this book argue and what other scholars have also found: digital literacy, agency, and citizenship education may be the most promising approach to promoting healthy digital engagement for learning, communication, and socialization. It may not be the quickest "fix" to our existing concerns, but in conjunction with interventions at multiple levels, it may help students and schools develop the beliefs and habits necessary for long-term success in a digital world. The growing public notion that solely banning cell phones in schools will fully address the complicated, interconnected effects of social media on our youth's development and well-being is alluring. It is possible that cell phone bans will address some issues we face in schools, but the research on this topic remains nascent. Instead, we join the authors in inviting you to resist oversimplified, one-size-fits-all messaging and approaches that promise quick fixes to the issue of social media use in our students' lives and consider embracing a different narrative. Wading into the messiness of digital media education and leveraging the capacities of social media for learning and engagement may be the most promising and empowering directions for the future of our youth.

Kathy C. Rohn
Assistant Research Professor
Department of Educational Leadership
University of Connecticut

Adam M. McCready
Assistant Professor-in-Residence
Department of Educational Leadership
University of Connecticut

Preface

Throughout the book, the "we" refers to the Meriden Public Schools, a mid-size urban district, and the Cheshire Public Schools, a suburban district, that have leveraged social media for school and district success. Regardless of district size or demographics, social media can play a role in your district.

Let us be clear: we do not support the unrestricted use of phones in the classroom. Let us be even clearer: we do not support a total ban on cell phones in our schools. Social media did not create bullying, attentional issues, or student anxiety. These issues were with us well before X, TikTok, and Snapchat, and they will be issues for schools and communities with or without cell phone bans. Schools must partner with students and families and work together to ensure reasonable screen time and appropriate use of social media.

We could not agree more with the teachers concerned about policies that ban devices, limit AI exposure, and restrict social media. Cell phone-free classrooms might sometimes be necessary, but we must also create opportunities for technology to be used in learning. Students need activities that require technology, engage them, foster collaboration, and prepare them for the world that lies ahead. Educational institutions must support innovation and prepare students for a rapidly changing world, as we still do not know exactly how technology will change future job prospects.

By educating all learners on the appropriate use of social media, we can take advantage of social media's many benefits to our students. Athletes are making connections with future college coaches; musicians and actors are posting their performances to enhance their opportunities; artists are displaying their work; schools are sharing timely information with students and families; students are marketing themselves to prospective employers and university admission officials, and students are connecting, dare we say, becoming friends with others in their local friend network and throughout the World Wide Web.

When asked in an interview what advice we have for other school districts to deal with social media issues, we responded simply, "We feel your pain!" Like any new tool, we must continue to educate students, staff, and families. We provide age-appropriate topics beginning in kindergarten. All students participate in digital citizenship lessons to help them make wise choices online and in life. Students learn about online privacy, creating a positive digital footprint, and how to be effective communicators in a digital world. Most recently, students are helping to design guidelines for the application of artificial intelligence.

Staff also participates in yearly professional development on online safety, data privacy, and cybersecurity. Families are invited to informative Internet Safety presentations with their students and events demonstrating technology's positive impact on student learning. We have found it very beneficial to ensure students, staff, and families hear the same message. We have also delivered helpful information at district-wide events, such as concerts, musicals, and sporting events.

Social media has provided a platform for students to enhance their college opportunities. In addition to the sports video clips and publicly shared statistics leading to connections with coaches and various athletic programs, students have shared their research, work endeavors, and community service experiences. Families also enjoy how social media can update scores during games, provide game schedules, share highlight reels of players, and post about awards and recognitions earned! Scenes from theater productions and missed solos have also been posted on social media to garner attention from college programs. Schools and districts can even livestream important events on various social media platforms to people around the globe.

While some superintendents have banned social media in their districts, others have leveraged social media channels to creatively connect with their communities and student constituents. Before making that decision, we ask that you explore how social media can help school systems with hiring, professional development, student learning, systems and operations, and building a positive school climate and culture.

Take the journey with us as we attempt to make connections with you.

Acknowledgments

We would like to acknowledge the Meriden Public Schools' and the Cheshire Public Schools' students, staff, and families who make us better educational leaders. A special thank you to our central office teams and union leaders for being great thought partners and teammates. We could not do this work without each and every one of you. Thank you to our dedicated and supportive Boards of Education who are committed to school district improvement and success. Also, a special thank you to the University of Connecticut's Department of School Leadership partners, Dr. Kathy Rohn and Dr. Adam McCready, for their contributions to public education.

Lastly, we want to acknowledge our students and staff who provided the social media stories, challenges, and successes. Through your courageous work, we learned so much and have a great deal to share with other school districts that want to maximize the benefits of social media for their students, staff, and stakeholders. Thank you for making our districts and schools great places to work, learn, innovate, and celebrate.

Social media has taken our nation by storm and has become a fixture in the lives of our students and families. A quick scan of the lunchroom or the sidelines of a school sporting event will demonstrate how integral the cell phone has become to daily activities. Parents and students have instant access to a myriad of information, whether actively seeking a specific item, scrolling through a news feed, or receiving notifications. While the printed flyer of an upcoming school presentation sits long forgotten in the bottom of a student's book bag, dozens of parents may see a social media post about the same event.

With estimates of over five billion social media users, or slightly more than half of the world's population, consuming social media content, our educational institutions must have a plan. In just over two years, we may now have over half of the world's population getting content from social media. Ignoring social media's reach and influence is no longer a viable option. Due to social media being present everywhere, it has quickly become a valuable tool for district improvement and success. Learn how social media can affect your school's and district's improvement efforts.

Let us deal with and address the elephant in the room before we share success stories occurring in school districts across the country. Leveraging social media to promote district and school success comes with challenges. Monitoring student behavior on social media platforms and the role school districts should play is still evolving. Schools nationwide are dealing with conflicts and issues brought into the schools due to something that occurred outside the school walls on social media platforms.

School social media guidelines should not be about punishing students but instead supporting them. Our goal must be to keep all students safe. There are many examples where professional staff intervened and provided the support their students needed. Whether districts begin social media monitoring programs or not, districts will be forced to deal with issues that started through inappropriate social media interactions.

The following examples illustrate how social media can impact the daily operations of a school district and its students:

A Day at the Zoo

Students were excited about their field trip to the local zoo. As the students entered the bus, the teacher checked off one name after another. You could not help but notice all the students on their phones. Of course, they were not making actual telephone calls. The phones represented their cameras and computers for the day. After about a forty-minute drive, the group arrived at the local zoo for a day of fun, exploration, and learning.

After visiting the lion exhibit and on their way to see the penguins, the teacher leading the trip received an urgent call from their school's principal. The teacher wondered, what could it possibly be? The trip was going smoothly; the students were well-behaved and were enjoying the day. Couldn't this call wait? No, the call could not wait! One of the students posted a picture of the lion on numerous social media networks. The only problem was the caption read, "Lion on the loose at the local zoo."

You can only imagine and speculate what difficulty and concern this post caused the school and the zoo. The student claimed it was an innocent post and genuinely felt terrible upon hearing of the concerns the post generated. While the student quickly removed the post, the damage was done. Despite the corrective actions, many parents and citizens were terrified and concerned. Once again, the school district was left to answer all the questions and face all the criticisms.

Keeping Schools Safe

School threats are being made and shared through social media channels across the country. Swatting is the effort to initiate a SWAT (Special Weapons and Tactics) response by sharing false information and has become a national phenomenon. In Connecticut alone, there have been fifty reported threats in a short three-week window. Many school communities have been handling multiple threats and working with local police officials who have brought in the FBI to identify the individuals responsible for the threat. Social media not only allows offenders to make threats without direct connection to them, but its broad reach allows these threats to be shared before the police can verify them or determine if they are credible.

Even worse for schools, police departments, and communities is the number of individuals reporting these messages. A general school threat in one part of the country can quickly be reported on social media, connecting it to a school or community in your home area. We experience the challenges of reporting vague school threats in our district. A national school threat message was circulating on social media networks when one of our parents reposted it and said her daughter "heard" it was geared toward her school in our district. This new report changed everything!

We spoke with the police chief, deputy chief, and captain. That simple report ended up on the local Facebook page. This national threat that had no direct connection to our school district was attributed to our community. Our local police department quickly visited the resident's home to talk with her and her daughter. Initially, the police officer received a cool reception from the mother and daughter.

After delicately explaining the seriousness of the situation and the potential consequences, the parent and child became more cooperative. The social media rampage was in full speed ahead. Parents shared the message, reported it, encouraged everyone to stay home from school, and questioned why school administrators did not send any official correspondence home. Some posts were full displays of parent rage at the school system. Comments like "Don't they care about the safety of our children?", "How could they just go to bed knowing these threats?", and "Fire them all—they are useless"!

After a quick home visit from the police, the picture became much clearer. Finally, we had the accurate information to share with our families. As the officer knocked on the family's door, he was greeted by a shocked parent and a confused student. As the mother invited the officer into her home, he quickly began questioning as his superiors anxiously awaited his report.

So here it is: the mom reposted the general threat with a comment above it, saying her daughter shared that this involved one of our city's schools. When the daughter was asked why she shared that and how she knew it involved a city school, she said, "Well, that's what my friends were saying." Needless to say, the police and school officials were not happy. A story shared by a student to her mom and a social media report with a comment attached had left a community afraid, angry, and confused. The school system quickly sent an electronic message to their families, but by now, it was almost 11:00 p.m.

Attendance was definitely impacted the next day, and too many students missed school for posts that had no connection to their school system. Rather than complain about social media or the parents and students, the school system created a communication plan about reporting threats to the authorities, not reposting them. The district also discussed how they could reinforce their message with the students during their advisory block.

This incident left us wondering how we could use the power of social media to get school and district messages sent, delivered, and read in a timely, cost-effective manner. Social media has not only delivered a message to families; it has created a forum for them to share their opinions. The only problem was that views were shared based on inaccurate and misleading information. How can we use that power safely, accurately, and openly to harness the voices of our entire school community?

College Bound

It was the last inning of the championship baseball game. The pitcher was clinging to a 1 to 0 lead, but the bases were loaded with two outs and a two-two count. As the pitcher kicked his leg up, reached his arm back, and delivered the ball to the catcher's mitt, everyone waited in anticipation as the umpire called ball three: one more pitch, one more challenge, and one more opportunity. Phones were recording these last pitches and, soon, posts would be all over social media.

The real triumph would not be the strike three that was called for the school's first-ever state championship banner, but rather how the posts about this game caught the attention of a college baseball coach who just happened to be looking for a great competitor who could round out his roster next year. Social media notably made this pitcher a local star. Still, more importantly, it helped him receive a college scholarship and the opportunity to continue playing the sport he grew up to love as a four-year-old in tee ball.

A Black Eye for the District

A picture of a young child with a large bruise and an almost closed swollen eye appeared on social media. The tagline, "This happened at school." Viewers were left to wonder if there was a fight. Did someone throw something at him? Is this school safe? Where were the teachers? How could this happen? Of course, outrage ensued! Post after post, the school became the target of the story. What was not shared until hours later was that the child fell off the playscape at one of the district's elementary schools. Also not shared on social media initially was that the child was with his babysitter after school hours using the school's playscape. In this case, immediate outrage quickly ended with deleted tweets, as additional tweets began supporting the school.

For some students, social media remains their connection to the outside world. While uncomfortable in the walls of their schools, where anxiety is high and self-esteem low, inside the boundaries of their computer screen exist opportunities for friendships worldwide. Their connections and friends often have similar interests and challenges, but all share the need to belong.

With all the negativity surrounding social media in general, one might wonder if schools and communities can use social media positively. Be aware and be careful, but also know that we have seen social media bring awareness to charitable causes and lift the spirits of communities across the nation. We have seen people learn new skills and share their areas of expertise. We have also seen people spread joy and bring happiness to others. We have been intrigued by bake-offs and recipe-sharing communities through social media channels.

School districts also effectively promote district events to all stakeholders through social media. The first day of school notices, snow day notifications, and open houses are promoted to students and families through social media and standard district notifications. The community is also alerted to Back to School Expos, College and Career Fairs, Financial Aid Seminars, and Technology Symposiums through standard district channels and social media networks.

Other school departments, such as school counseling, have engaged and informed parents and students about upcoming events through social media. Food and Nutrition Services have promoted their universal free breakfast and lunch programs for all students. Food menus, summer food sites, and job opportunities are also promoted by Food and Nutrition Services through social media channels.

Videos are a powerful way to learn how to complete tasks and share sports and other performance clips. Innovative teachers are taking advantage of this opportunity by having their students use

FIGURE 1.1. Financial aid. *Source:* Francis T. Maloney School Counselors, August 9, 2024.

FIGURE 1.2. Food and Nutrition Services. *Source:* Meriden Public Schools Food & Nutrition Services, June 16, 2025.

the platform to present projects and meet course requirements. As for these social media challenges, how many of our teens have participated in at least one?

Social media provides numerous videos geared toward sharing information or teaching others. How can this social media outlet positively impact education and student engagement? Students can explore subject matter and content that is most interesting to them, learn new things, perfect personal skills, and get assistance with homework. Students and others can also use social media as a social outlet tool to connect and communicate with others, near and far.

Students regularly support their friends by liking their posts and sharing positive comments about them. Different video posts can help our students understand and be more empathetic to differences of opinion. Some videos are also encouraging and motivational. Students have also used social media to gain employment, study for tests, complete assignments, address health matters, and deal with loneliness.

Before you decide to create social media accounts for your district, meet with your leadership team and discuss the following:

- What is your brand? When creating social media accounts, you want to secure the same or similar account names across platforms. To do this, you may need to add a state abbreviation, zip code, school mascot, or other identifying information if your district's name is already in use. For example, @MiddletownPS is the Twitter/X account for the Middletown Public Schools in Middletown, Connecticut, and @MiddletownOH is the account for Middletown City Schools in Ohio. Try to select something that will make sense in your community.
- Who is your audience? Are you trying to improve your communication with your students? Staff? Parents? Other community stakeholders? Do your parents, families, and community support it and use it?
- What platforms are your target audiences already using? Determine which platform you will use to meet your various stakeholders. For example, despite its origins in college culture, Facebook has become known as a platform for adults rather than students. If you are trying to reach your adult stakeholders, Facebook or X may be the perfect option. However, if you are trying to reach younger stakeholders, YouTube, TikTok, Snapchat, or Instagram are better options. If you publish your message to platforms that don't reach your target audience, your efforts to improve communication will be unsuccessful.
- Who will control content? Who is the trusted person on your team who will consistently share the district's message? This may be the superintendent in smaller districts, while a communications team may share the responsibility in larger districts. Have a point person to control the content and frequency of posts, encourage the community to enhance its use, and focus on the actual video posts.

- Will each school within your district have its own social media accounts, or will principals and school staff be asked to submit content to a district point person? If schools have their accounts, how will the district monitor this? Will schools be required to mention the district in any posts (@districtname) or use a hashtag (#districttagline) that is easily searchable?
- How often will content be posted? Be realistic and keep it manageable. You may want to start with once a week and increase posts as you become more comfortable using the platforms. However, if you publicize that you will post every Monday, make sure you do. Set a calendar reminder to ensure the message is sent out. If you want to build a following, you need to provide timely content and stick to any promised schedule.
- What will you post? We will provide additional examples in the following chapters, but here are a few ideas to start your thinking:
  - Important dates—Back to School, Parent Nights and Open Houses, school vacations, end of marking periods, exam schedules, report cards
  - Celebrations—Awards received by students, staff, sports teams, and academic accomplishments
  - Special Events—Musicals, school plays, concerts, ribbon cuttings, college signings, field day
  - Student or staff profiles—Highlight a member of your school community and what they contribute every day
  - Blooper reels—It is all right if a video isn't perfect. Sharing your mistakes humanizes you as a leader and reinforces what education is all about: learning from your mistakes. When you get a problem wrong in math class, success and joy come from figuring out your mistake and getting it right.

Social media, like our educators, has gotten a bad rap from some constituents, but both are necessary for us to have successful, productive education systems to prepare tomorrow's leaders. Any social media action plan for your schools or district must include ways for students to protect their privacy. Schools must

FIGURE 1.3. CT high school theatre festival. *Source:* Marisa Volo, March 4, 2023.

avoid mistakes that could lead to privacy concerns. School officials should also know how apps share personal data and use device settings to guard student information. Schools should also ensure that their students respect others' online privacy. As educators, parents, and students have become more social media savvy, major players like Meta have changed their advertisement structure to ensure that their apps are age-appropriate.

While social media can be overwhelming at first, it's not going away, so schools should reap the benefits of its popularity and reach. Social media videos and hashtag campaigns are becoming more and more popular. Staff use their phone's camera to highlight student and school success stories. With so many social media options at the user's fingertips, a school district new to the social media scene should build success with one platform before expanding to multiple possibilities.

This brief overview of social media platforms describes the various platforms available:

YouTube: https://www.youtube.com/

YouTube is a video platform owned by Google. School districts can create a channel to house all district-related videos and playlists and group them into areas of interest. Examples of videos a school district may post include board meetings, sporting events, messages from the superintendent, and special events such as graduation and awards ceremonies. To set up an account, visit https://www.youtube.com/creators/how-things-work/getting-started

The terms of service for YouTube may be found at https://www.youtube.com/static?template=terms

Facebook: https://www.facebook.com/

Facebook, owned by Meta, allows users to post photos, videos, and text. Others may like, comment, and/or share the information. While originally developed for use by college students, Facebook is now known for being used by an older audience. The ability to post text with a photo or video makes Facebook a good option for sharing special events or examples of school daily activities, including assemblies, town meetings, and instructional activities. To set up an account, visit https://www.facebook.com/help/188157731232424

The terms of service for Facebook may be found at https://www.facebook.com/terms.php?_rdr

Instagram: https://www.instagram.com/

While users may add text to Instagram posts, it is primarily used for sharing photos and videos, known as "reels." In addition to adding posts to your feed, you can create a "story," which is content only available for twenty-four hours. Meta also owns Instagram. To set up an Instagram account, visit https://help.instagram.com/424737657584573/?helpref=related_articles

The terms of service for Instagram are available at https://help.instagram.com/581066165581870/.

X (formerly known as Twitter): https://x.com/

X shares short messages, videos, and links to other content. Unless you are a premium subscriber, the limit for X posts is 280 characters, up from 140 when Twitter originated. Elon Musk owns X. The character limits make X a good option for sharing short messages such as school delays and closings, upcoming events, and sporting event updates and results. To create an account on X, visit https://help.x.com/en/using-x/create-x-account. X's terms of service can be found at https://x.com/en/tos

Threads: https://www.threads.net/

Like X, Threads is used to share short messages, videos, and links to other content. It is owned by Meta, and users must have an Instagram account. Information on setting up a Threads account can be found at https://help.instagram.com/1747515265645443. The Threads terms of service are available at https://help.instagram.com/769983657850450.

Pinterest: https://www.pinterest.com/

Pinterest is used to share images, videos, and infographics. It is popular among teachers for sharing lesson plans, bulletin board designs, and classroom organization ideas. Pinterest is a publicly traded company cofounded by entrepreneur Ben Silbermann. To create a Pinterest account, visit https://help.pinterest.com/en/article/get-a-pinterest-account. Pinterest's terms of service may be found at https://policy.pinterest.com/en

LinkedIn: https://www.linkedin.com/feed/

LinkedIn is a platform used to share information, ideas, and opportunities. It can be a valuable resource in recruiting staff members and allows potential candidates to highlight their work experience. LinkedIn is owned by Microsoft. For information on creating a LinkedIn profile, visit https://www.linkedin.com/help/linkedin/answer/a1338223/signing-up-to-join-linkedin. LinkedIn's terms of service may be found at https://www.linkedin.com/legal/l/service-terms.

The social media sites listed below are not commonly used for school district messaging but are being used by members of school communities, so they are included here.

TikTok: https://www.tiktok.com/en/

TikTok is known for sharing short, trendy videos, some of which have led to disruptive "challenges" that have made their way into school systems, including stealing items from school and destroying school property. TikTok is owned by Chinese company ByteDance, which has led to privacy concerns. To create a TikTok account, visit https://support.tiktok.com/en/getting-started/creating-an-account. TikTok's terms of service may be found at: https://www.tiktok.com/legal/page/us/terms-of-service/en

Snapchat: https://www.snapchat.com/

Snapchat may be used to share photos, videos, text, and drawings. "Snaps" famously disappear after being viewed by the recipient, but this temporary nature is misleading as recipients can screenshot messages. Chats may be visible for twenty-four hours to seven days, depending on the setting options. Information on creating a Snapchat account can be found at https://help.snapchat.com/hc/en-us/articles/7012333136788-How-to-Create-a-Snapchat-Account. Snapchat's terms of service are available at: https://snap.com/en-US/terms

Reddit: https://www.reddit.com/

Reddit is a discussion board where users can share photos, videos, text, ratings, and links. Information on creating a Reddit account can be found at https://support.reddithelp.com/hc/en-us/articles/360060420092-How-do-I-sign-up-for-a-Reddit-account. Reddit's terms of service can be found at https://www.redditinc.com/policies/user-agreement

Discord: https://discord.com/

Discord allows users to communicate through text, voice, and video chat. Information on creating a Discord account can be found at https://support.discord.com/hc/en-us/articles/360033931551-Getting-Started. Discord's terms of service are available at https://discord.com/terms

BeReal: https://bereal.com/en/

Users are prompted to share an unfiltered photo on BeReal once a day using both the rear and front-facing cameras to capture what is really happening. For information on creating a BeReal account, visit https://help.bereal.com/hc/en-us/categories/7209052114973-The-Guide. BeReal's terms of service may be found at https://bereal.com/en/terms/

Social media providers have been connected to national security and privacy concerns at all levels, leaving us wondering what role social media should play in our nation's classrooms. We have seen social media inspire, engage, and challenge students with complicated academic skills. Still, social media challenges put students and staff at risk and in potential danger.

Can common ground be found with such popular social media platforms? With so many American teenagers using social media, there is no question that it has become an integral part of teens' lives. Students can use social media for homework assistance and test preparation. Videos on social media can also inform and instruct students, build relationships with students, and help us connect with families and stakeholders. A good rule to follow when using social media vehicles is only to post your message if you would be comfortable with it appearing on the front page of the local newspaper or a billboard on the local interstate highway.

Most schools nationwide have experienced disruptions from various social media challenges. These challenges have revealed the need for students to seek opportunities to connect with others. While some challenges can be fun and harmless, students must develop the skills to distinguish between safe and harmful, as well as appropriate and hurtful. Students need to be taught how to use social media to support their learning, connect with others, and promote their profiles to potential colleges and future employers.

Every day, there is another controversial article about the daily challenges of social media in school systems. While some superintendents have banned social media in their district, others have leveraged social media channels to connect with their communities and constituents creatively. Authentic videos on social media platforms have proven to be a powerful approach for messaging across schools and districts. These engaging apps keep users in a session for multiple minutes.

Most striking is that TikTok, while used most frequently by teens and those under thirty, boasts that half of its active users are over thirty. Social media's personal and informal approach can create a casual, cost-effective community engagement space for your school district or a governor looking to ban cell phones from schools rather than address student behavior and mental health needs. Cell phones are an easy target! They connect users to their personal AI assistance and the uncertain world of social media. Rather than teach students how to use the power of their cell phones appropriately, some governors are garnering news media by proposing cell phone bans.

Other governors are directing school systems to specific companies to purchase cell phone bag lockers. This should not surprise us. People are looking for a quick fix and an easy solution, someone to take the blame, so why not choose a cell phone? It appears that states across the nation are banning cell phones at school as a way to address the ongoing youth mental health crisis rather than enlisting the support of social workers, psychologists, and other support staff.

Do they realize that school is only six hours a day and only one hundred eighty days a year? Our students' issues do not just occur at schools. Too often, issues in the community have nothing to do with school and take up a tremendous amount of staff time. Time that should be spent on teaching and learning. Our schools can be the catalyst to show students developmentally appropriate ways to use social media effectively and how to enhance their digital profile.

We must share the risks and make recommendations for safe usage. Social media abuses have flourished, as others have used online harassment and abuse to discriminate and sexually exploit others. This is a significant problem that needs community attention, especially from schools. Schools' new role and responsibility is to prepare students for a successful life in careers that may still need to be created. So, rather than banning cell phones, let's educate staff, students, and families so they can support their children.

Circumstances are straining an already under-resourced and understaffed system, especially for psychologists, social workers, school nurses, and student counselors. Many school systems have partnered with safety management providers to ensure posts on their school networks referencing violence or self-harm are dealt with timely and efficiently. While just about all school districts monitor student activity on their network, some communities expect their school system to monitor student behavior on social media, whether accessed during school hours or after school hours.

The latest trend is for districts to pay contractors to monitor student social media usage and internal technology to alert school officials when red flags go up. With limited research on the program's effectiveness and civil rights advocates expressing concerns, school systems are tiptoeing around what the role and responsibility of the school system is and should be. School systems fear that student safety will be jeopardized if they don't step in and provide support.

Chicago Public Schools began a social media monitoring program in 2020 with the support of a $750,000 grant from the United States Department of Justice. The Chicago program has its share of supporters and critics. School districts care about their students and want to help them and their families. We are left wondering how politicians, influencers, and businesses with limited relationships with students can guide their social media usage. Social media has been and continues to be used for threats and false accusations. It is up to us to monitor, assess, and address these threats in a timely and supportive manner.

School social media guidelines should not be about punishing students but instead supporting them. Our goal must be to keep all other students safe. There are many examples where professional staff intervened and provided the support their students needed. Whether districts begin social media monitoring programs or not, districts will be forced to deal with issues that started through inappropriate social media interactions.

Banning social media, restricting friend sites, and limiting screen time may create unintended harm to our most fragile students. The headlines read, "Virginia School District Latest to Ban Phones in Classrooms" (The Virginia Gazette, August 23, 2024), "Philadelphia Parents, Schools Debate Details of Phone Bans" (The Philadelphia Inquirer, August 26, 2024), and "CT Schools Could Lock Up Students' Cell Phones Under Policy Proposed by the State Board of Education," (CT Insider, August 19, 2024). On the heels of big cities like New York City and Los Angeles, community leaders have banned cell phones.

The rationale for these bans continues to leave unanswered questions. Will the ban make students engaged, rid our students of anxiety that their social media decisions are causing, and stop AI-induced cheating? Requiring students, staff, and schools to allocate time and resources to locking up phones will not solve our children's problems. A balanced approach that clearly delineates when cell phones should be off and put away is a great place to start.

Rather than spending time creating homework assignments that AI can complete in seconds, people are advocating for cell phone bans and anti-AI campaigns. AI is not the cause of cheating! Cheating often correlates with more difficult work and higher stakes for achievement. Yet, despite the views of some, AI cheating is difficult to detect accurately and prove beyond doubt. We aim to get teachers to use AI to tackle their workload more efficiently and get students to think at higher levels. AI in education is not something that might occur years into the future. It is something impacting us right now and is a future certainty. To make this work in our schools, we must look at teaching technologies, learning tasks, and curriculum assessments differently.

With all the focus on banning cell phones, we must share how teachers use them to access AI to enhance their students' learning. We know how many tech-savvy high school teachers are showing their students how to use AI to improve their writing for successful futures. One teacher introduced ChatGPT, only to realize that her class was well aware and familiar with the platform. Educators must be futurists who prepare their students for a rapidly changing world. Teachers can teach their students how to use AI ethically and advantageously. Teacher efforts have revealed improved writing and increased student engagement. Yet, engagement is the most common reason for banning cell phones in our schools.

Teachers surprise their students with innovative assignments by incorporating their cell phones, AI, and social media into learning tasks. We need educators who push the envelope, move the needle, and create the graduates our nation needs. Senior graduates need to leave our schools with a working knowledge of using AI and social media to their advantage. Employers are searching for candidates with strong technology and AI skills. Technology skills are becoming more important in so many careers.

Students must also learn how to differentiate between fact and fiction, especially as deep fakes created using artificial intelligence become more prevalent in rural, suburban, and urban communities. This is one area where schools and educators can play a helpful role and provide necessary education, mentoring, and training. Schools and their staff have already built positive relationships and trust with students. This has positioned them well to educate our children in appropriate social media behavior.

Many educators have already begun to change their teaching practices to account for students using the AI assistant in the palm of their hand on their cell phones. Teachers are requiring drafts of work, presentations, interviews, photos, supervised writing, and personal reflections. Those same teachers use their AI assistants to help with lesson planning, assignment creation, test correction, language translation, data analysis, and immediate student feedback.

Data reveal that the average teacher who uses AI saves thirteen hours a week on routine work. Even more importantly, teachers who use AI to save planning time gain time to focus on their best teaching and most engaging instructional practices. We mustn't let the fear of social media distractions cause bans on cell phones and severe AI restrictions from our schools. Again, a balanced approach can meet the needs of our students and staff.

Many workers in various fields use AI in their workplace. The reasons for using AI include saving time so they can focus on more complex work and collaborative tasks. Many workers also believe AI expands their creativity and allows them to think outside the box. For these reasons, it is imperative that our public schools appropriately leverage technology, including cell phones. Many employees have clearly stated that hiring candidates with AI exposure and experience are key elements in the job decision process.

Rather than banning social media in our schools, educational institutions should take the lead and teach students about appropriate boundaries, self-reflection, building their positive brand, and avoiding the fear of missing out (FOMO). College students continue to adopt AI in their school programs. Our experiences have shown us that a large percentage of teachers and students are using AI to support their work. Despite this impressive usage by our teaching staff and high school students, many teachers and their unions are leading the charge to ban cell phones. Our cell phones are portable devices that open the door to countless AI options.

Educational institutions must embrace AI and teach students how to navigate this new learning tool safely and successfully. K–12 public schools must prepare students to use their cell phones to navigate social media's vast influence and the possibilities of AI. AI technology allows students to research, summarize information, and create course study guides. College students continue to adopt AI in their school programs; however, regulations, guidance, and support are still needed.

Canadian Prime Minister Justin Trudeau famously stated at the 2018 World Economic Forum, "The pace of change has never been this fast, yet it will never be this slow again." The digitization of our politics, economy, and social life is already here. Blanket bans on cell phones, AI, and social media won't work; we will leave our teens ill-prepared for future workplaces. Let's adopt a balanced approach that educates our teens on appropriate usage.

Inappropriate social media challenges have forced schools nationwide to cancel school days and other extracurricular activities. In addition, these challenges have encouraged vandalism and vilifying behaviors. Of great concern is that some social media accounts keep users anonymous. This leaves schools and authorities powerless to address offenders and provide necessary consequences. Most troubling is that these challenges have left students emotionally and physically hurt.

So what can our students' parents do to support their children? Parents can be actively involved in their child's online presence by being aware of age requirements and safety precautions. Most importantly, parents must teach their children the difference between appropriate and inappropriate social media use. Caution: children should not share personal information online, especially when it is solicited from an unknown source, and parents should monitor what is being shared.

Parents should also be aware of the amount and speed of information coming to their children from social media outlets. Schools can offer parent training seminars to ensure that school officials and parents are on the same page regarding safe social media use by children. A unified front between schools and parents is required. While school policies and guidelines may help during the school day, ultimately, students need monitoring outside school hours as well.

Education professionals want better outcomes for their students. The need to do better is well documented in headline news—fewer students attend school, standardized test scores are dropping, and incidents that reflect poor student mental health are rising. Administrators and teachers research curricula, disaggregate data, attend conferences and workshops, and spend hours planning strategies to address issues in their school systems. Even in high-performing districts, teachers and administrators want better outcomes for more students.

To identify areas for improvement and strategies to achieve goals, districts and schools turn to creating comprehensive improvement plans. Improvement plans will vary from district to district and school to school, but at the core, they are all focused on improving student outcomes. While the strategies may differ, there is one tool that can support and advance improvement efforts, and that is social media. Social media provides a vast network and multiple measures to reach stakeholders efficiently regarding both cost and time.

Social media can support school improvement efforts in two overarching ways. First, it is a vehicle to let your community know what is happening in the school system and how they can contribute and participate. Schools need to build transparency and trust with parents, teachers, students, and other stakeholders. If you don't tell your story, someone else will. Be proactive and control the narrative. Second, social media can be a resource to inform district and school actions. What are other people doing? What might work for you? Have others tried something that just doesn't seem to work, or is there a great idea that appears to be a perfect fit for your district? Take it to social media, do your research, and find the answers you are looking for.

It is important to note that since beginning work on this book, Facebook has become Meta and introduced Threads in response to Twitter. Meanwhile, Twitter has become X. By the time this goes to print, there will likely be new versions of existing platforms and entirely new platforms that leverage artificial intelligence to communicate with users. District leaders must be prepared to adapt their leadership strategies to ensure they are reaching the desired audience.

In the following chapters, we will discuss ideas for leveraging social media to advance district improvement goals. These strategies can easily be applied at the school level as well. Join us as we share our journey of hiring social, learning social, celebrating social, leveraging social, and leading social. Not all strategies will work for all districts, but we hope you find something to make the path to district improvement easier.

Social media can be a major component of a school system's teacher recruitment efforts and help them increase their candidate pool, expand the depth and quality of candidates, and help fill staff shortage areas. Like any teacher recruitment effort, schools must know their audience and be clear about whom they are trying to recruit. Share your vision, make the hiring process simple and user-friendly, and express why your district is a great place to work and build a professional career. These efforts will help attract quality candidates looking to work in a positive, supportive environment.

Do candidates regularly look to social media to find their next job? Based on our experience and numerous conversations with recent hires, we know that many school systems are filling job openings through social media posts. If you're not on social media, you may miss out because candidates may not see you. Social media also helps you spread the word that your district is a great place to work, whether starting your career or looking for a new venture. Social media is also easy to use and a cost-effective recruitment strategy.

District officials share job openings, promotion opportunities, extracurricular and coaching positions, and professional learning experiences through social media networks.

Social media has become an active recruitment tool for Fortune 500 companies, not-for-profit organizations, neighborhood businesses, and our schools. How can schools find and hire the best candidates through social media channels?

Once your audience is defined, it is time to clarify the benefits of working in your district. What separates you from other districts? It could be salary, professional learning opportunities, relationships with your union and staff, new facilities, a supportive board of education, engaged families, or a reputation for innovation and success. Can you share testimonials and endorsements from students, staff, recent graduates, families, business partners, or community agencies? One district launched an online Distinguished Alumni Program. Past alumni were featured on the district website and through various social media channels.

Social media allows school systems to highlight their district climate and culture. Visuals of your school community may attract current and future candidates. The benefits of using social media for educator recruitment include building awareness about your school district, allowing communication with other educators, providing a forum to understand a diverse candidate pool, and saving money on costly traditional teacher recruitment efforts.

Districts looking to use social media for staff recruitment would benefit from setting clear, attainable goals, selecting the most appropriate social media platform, expanding their social media reach, and sharing the success of their efforts through various social media networks. Social media can broaden the audience for those job postings and share why your district is where candidates should want to work. In essence, social media can bring your school and district to life.

Social media can help recruit and reach non-traditional talent pools—instead of a local newspaper circulation reaching one town, one post can now be seen by numerous audiences—locally, regionally, nationally, and internationally. When exploring why social media matters to your school district's recruitment efforts, it is hard to ignore the large percentage of candidates utilizing social media to find their next position. We know that teaching candidates want to work for districts that provide support, offer advancement opportunities, have strong, competent leaders, and possess a positive school climate and culture.

In the aftermath of the pandemic, the Cheshire Public Schools had several open paraeducator positions like most districts. They committed to holding a job fair in an effort to recruit non-certified positions. There wasn't a budget for television, and print had experienced a decline in market penetration.

Social media was employed to get the word out. Cheshire tends to hire non-certified people via word of mouth. The superintendent sent an email notifying staff of the impending job fair and encouraged them to follow his Instagram and the District's Instagram and Facebook feeds. District employees were asked to repost their advertisements for the job fair. If they sent in a screenshot of their post, they were entered to win one of three $25 gift cards.

The post was among Cheshire's most engaged campaigns in its history, resulting in great leads for non-certified positions. It wasn't even that applicants always saw the post, but they heard about the fair from someone who did. Social media not only gave tremendous reach at nearly zero cost, but it also supported a team culture among staff. It is that team atmosphere that will inspire current and future staff.

FIGURE 2.1. MPS hiring. *Source:* Meriden Public Schools Food & Nutrition Services, February 6, 2025.

Social media is beneficial when trying to diversify the candidate pool to reflect our student population. We can reach students in Historically Black Colleges and Universities (HBCUs), share visit information with prospective students, and reach other areas outside the continental United States. Several neighboring districts have successfully recruited teacher candidates from Puerto Rico. EdTech Chats can help share best practices, while EdWeb helps share resources, classroom settings, and management strategies.

Postings can attract top talent, reach people not actively looking for a job, source passive candidates, and let the prospective candidate become familiar with the culture of the district or organization. School systems can share the good news about their

FIGURE 2.2. CPS hiring fair. *Source:* Cheshire Public Schools, November 11, 2024.

hiring and attract other candidates, promote innovative activities in the district, share back-to-school messages, and inspire others to hold similar events. Engaging the employees lets your staff know they are valued members of your organization. By celebrating their accomplishments and sharing their good work, you can attract new employees and let others know that your organization is one where employees are respected and their contributions are valued.

As the demands of the teaching profession and the job market have changed, attracting and retaining qualified staff members has become one of the most significant challenges in education. Open positions posted to the district and state job websites that used to garner dozens, if not hundreds, of applications now return inquiries in the single digits. And, in some cases, no candidates at all. Educational institutions must find new ways to connect with a shrinking candidate pool. Social media is a great place to start.

Technology has undoubtedly redefined hiring processes in the business and education sectors. Years ago, districts would simply post on the district website, place an ad in the local newspaper, or post on a statewide education website. A recent job posting for a desktop support specialist went unanswered for weeks, using traditional hiring practices, until it was posted on social media.

Over a dozen responses led to three qualified candidates being hired. It stands to reason that if you continue to recruit using the methods you have always used in the past, you should not be surprised that your candidate pools are so limited. To diversify your workforce, you need to diversify your recruitment methods. Given the limited number of candidates and the market's competitive nature, districts must approach this creatively. Social media has already shown that it can help.

Local newspaper advertisements must provide more exposure to attract high-quality candidates. Local print newspapers, if still in business, have limited distribution networks. Again, districts can reach candidates locally, regionally, nationally, and internationally through social media platforms. A wide range of candidates allows the district to interview a diverse group of individuals. A pool of candidates that reflects the student population is vital to all districts. Covid-19 challenges and Zoom efficiencies have made connecting with candidates accessible anytime and anywhere.

Social media posts can build excitement and share information with potential staff members when visiting college campuses to recruit future graduates. Reminders about when you will be on campus, the time, and the location will be welcomed to ensure your district's immediate recognition. Building excitement when your district is interviewing on-site outside of your local region, outside of the continental United States, or internationally can happen through social media usage. Share interesting tidbits about your district and your supportive staff members. Share photos of your district and highlights of your community. It really is that simple!

By sharing a welcoming portrayal of your community, you can attract candidates from non-traditional talent pools or those not looking for a career change or new position. Does the fall color of New England resonate with someone? Do the blue skies and nearby beaches sound attractive to someone who has bitter-cold winters? Or does a quiet suburban community sound like a great change from the hustle and bustle of city life? Location does play a factor when selecting employment opportunities. Be sure to leverage your community's highlights when actively recruiting staff and use social media to share video footage.

Everyone wants to work in a district that values and respects its employees. Social media allows districts to share staff achievements and attract equally motivated new staff members. Post awards achieved by individuals or the district on social media. Recognize staff for academic excellence, student growth, and good work. Highlight support staff members and their contributions to the district. Make people feel part of the team. Send a clear message that all team members' contributions are valued.

At the beginning of the school year, posts about new teacher orientation are a great way to ensure a successful start to the school year. Highlights of the Week can include information from district staff, a welcome from the Board of Education President, and even lunch with a pizza truck from the teachers' union. Positive comments and likes from the new staff members get the school year off to the right start and convey the message that your schools are the place to be.

Did you recognize staff members at a board meeting for meeting or exceeding growth targets on the latest state assessment? Send a tweet, post a photo to Instagram, or leverage whatever social media platform your district uses. Have you just named your district Teacher of the Year? Celebrate the person with your district's social media channels. Build your Teacher of the Year profile and position them for statewide recognition. People inside the organization will be energized, and the outside community will quickly get a positive impression of your organization.

Don't forget classified staff accomplishments, such as the Paraprofessional of the Year or recognition for your food services or maintenance departments. Did your clerical staff union hold a team-building Paint Night? Post their masterpieces and demonstrate to potential employees that they will find a level of collegiality in your district that they may not find elsewhere. Too often, education efforts focus solely on certified staff. Don't forget to honor, celebrate, and recruit classified and support staff through social media.

FIGURE 2.3. Teachers of the year. *Source:* Meriden Public Schools, June 2024.

In later chapters, we will discuss celebrating student achievements, but highlighting your students' accomplishments is also attractive to prospective staff candidates. It demonstrates that in your district, students have the opportunity to succeed and are celebrated for it. Potential candidates see the good things happening in your district and want to become members of an organization with a positive and supportive culture. Social media posts and videos uniquely make people feel part of the event even though they were not there.

Districts looking to begin a social media campaign should start the process by doing an inventory of their current website. Does your current website provide information for potential candidates, including the hiring process, contractual benefits, and information about their district's climate and culture? Does the website share photographs and ideas to engage visitors? Once your website is ready to go, be sure to select the right social media platform to meet your intended audience. Refrain from giving in to the pressure to launch an easy social media option that is available to you. Clarify your audience and message, and choose a social media option to meet your needs.

Some districts that begin social media campaigns have also realized that their reach could be improved if they utilize boosts or post social media advertisements. Also, districts have partnered with their local newspaper providers to help run their social media campaigns. Prepared messages can be posted on the newspaper's social media pages. This provides time savings to the district and greatly expands the reach of their social media campaign.

As this last election cycle has come and passed, we have seen how effectively campaigns have used social media to share their messages. Social media provided campaigns with a cost-effective method of communicating with their constituents. Social media has also allowed our students and staff members to post their feelings or views on the election's outcomes. Student posts have resulted in back-and-forth taunts that have escalated to actual fights in schools. These incidents indicate that our students must be educated on appropriate social media use.

Even more troubling is that some teachers vent their election frustrations and other feelings through social media. These posts have ranged from expressing disappointment to threatening and soliciting fights. These posts again confirm the need for teacher and school staff professional learning about appropriate social media usage. Does your school system have appropriate social media usage policies, guidelines, or recommendations? Are your faculty educated in their free speech limitations? These are important questions to ask yourself as a leader.

Potential new hires can also learn about the district through vehicles such as Facebook Live. Have your Human Resources Director share the opportunities available in your district from the school or classroom where the positions are open. Highlight the resources a teacher choosing your district will enjoy. Show them a bright, sunny classroom with plenty of materials, a comfortable staff lounge, and ample parking. Post a video of a current new teacher showing why she chose your district and what she enjoys most about her work.

The video posted on social media of a recent college graduate from the state's premier university was gaining traction and garnering great attention. The teacher was with an enthusiastic third-grade class in the district's newly designed and launched Genius Lab. Students collaborated at their workstations as they created a day of experience on a visually crafted roadway for their Ozobots.

The short video showed a cool classroom designed to excite students, foster teamwork, and fuel critical thinking among all learners. The teacher operated as a facilitator as she supported students who were busy working in small groups. The teacher answered clarifying questions, offered guidance, and challenged students to lean on each other for answers. As the video post went viral locally, the school was thrilled, the university was honored, the teacher was praised, the families appreciated it, and the students were excited.

As for the district, they became the big winners. This video post revealed a great classroom for learning, a confident new teacher, engaged students, an exciting curriculum, and a safe place for learning and exploration. Without spending a dime on hiring ads or district-promoted puff pieces, this district reaped the benefits of an authentic social media post. The Personnel Office saw an increase in teacher applications and received a call from the university to expand college and district partnerships.

What sets your district apart? Why should a candidate choose your district over another? Social media allows you to show potential hires in real-time and repeatedly, not just tell them once. Leveraging technology throughout the hiring process also creates the expectation that technology is used in the district. The right candidate will be comfortable replying to online posts and submitting screening questions via video. Candidates can think about their responses, put their best foot forward, and know they are joining a district where technology integration supports productivity and district efficiency.

Another district now has candidates submit initial interview questions through brief video responses. This process allows candidates to think more deeply about their answers and eliminates the nerves that come with formal in-person interviews. A video interview allows the interview team to view videos at a time most convenient for them and enables them to review and listen again to a candidate's response.

Social media can also help your district and schools ensure they select candidates that reflect their values. You have modernized your hiring practices and are getting qualified candidates to apply, and you have incorporated video interviews for round one of the process. Now, it's time to ensure your candidate meets the professional and personal standards of the district. Rather than launching just a simple Google search of the staff finalist, check the candidate's social media feeds to make sure the employee represents the values of the district and is a good role model for your students. Are they truly role models for your students?

After you have made the job offer, celebrate that this educator has decided to join your team. It shows that you value your employees and work together to improve student outcomes.

It is another golden opportunity to build your brand. Take a picture of that new hire in front of district signage. Flood your social media channels with the celebratory photo.

Undoubtedly, social media has helped us recruit and retain staff members. However, staff utilization of their social media platforms has led to unwanted employee recognition and warning signs for all staff members. Years ago, a teacher was on medical leave for an extended period. While a substitute teacher did their best to keep the third-grade class on track and learning, the teacher on leave continued to expand her personal business. Social media allowed the teacher to broaden their soap and fragrance businesses.

Social media posts showed the staff member at company events, trade forums, fairs, and holiday bazaars. While social media drove up company sales, it also alerted the school district about a team member's violations of her medical leave. A brief meeting with the team member and the district led to an immediate investigation. The district had all the information it needed from numerous posts on many social media networks to sever its ties with the employee for misuse of company time.

Recently, an employee was accused of running a real estate business during the school workday. A quick review of district device usage and her social media posts with times of postings quickly cleared her of any wrongdoing. Staff members must know they can use social media to promote their students on school and district social media channels. Also, staff members must receive training on how to use their personal social media accounts safely and appropriately. Social media use has become a topic in new teacher inductions, meetings with teacher groups, administrator meetings, and Board of Education retreats.

Once the district has invested the financial and human capital in the recruitment and hiring process, the next challenge is to keep those candidates in your district. Ensuring staff members have opportunities to grow professionally is a vital retention strategy, especially for urban districts, where the pay may be lower than in wealthier, suburban districts. Find ways to support your staff members' dreams, and they will support your students and schools.

The last time you didn't know how to fix something in your home, what did you do? If you are like many others, you probably took to the Internet, and more than likely ended up on YouTube watching a how-to video that showed you step-by-step how to change and replace the headlight in your car, learn the latest dance moves, or match the perfect paint color. How we receive and consume information has changed in today's busy world. Social media provides bite-sized pieces of information that address immediate interests or concerns. This is true for staff professional development as well. Let social media enhance and enrich your professional learning experiences.

Just as our students may feel anxiety, insecurity, and fear from their social media presence, so too may teachers. Teachers may feel pressured to present a social media image that makes them popular with their students and portrays them as innovative, student-centered educators. Teachers are left to question what pictures or viewpoints they should post on their social media channels. With many educators posting photos and videos of their beautifully decorated classrooms or unique, engaging lesson delivery, other teachers must compete to meet their new social media standards, especially in the same school, district, or state.

Another challenge teachers may experience is the pressure to post about their students and classroom and the reactions their posts may receive. Teachers are too often left on their own to decide the appropriateness of their posts. While some teachers use social media to connect with their peers and share best teaching practices, other teachers may feel less confident and, at times, inferior. Teachers have expressed strong opinions about grading, the importance of parent involvement, the need for improved test scores, and the challenges of societal problems.

These posts have led to their colleagues disagreeing gently with their views or, in some cases, parent and community member complaints. If we ask our educators to share their students' excellent work through social media, we must provide them with the support they need to avoid social media pitfalls. Our educators have a stressful enough job; let's not allow social media to add more.

The spread of social media has reached teachers' professional development and learning. Social media has allowed teachers to share course lessons and teaching strategies. While social media usage makes people think of social networking and entertainment, it certainly has great value for professional collegiality and quality instruction. Schools and districts looking to use social media for professional learning should build a trusting network.

Some districts have called on their student experts to provide professional learning experiences for their staff. With most students having cell phones by age thirteen, we know that our students have recently experienced navigating the world of social media. These students recognize and appreciate that technology will continue to be a part of their lives and learning. Many of our students have become experts and have used technology and social media successfully for years. So, in addition to having older students teach younger students about the appropriate use of technology, these students can deliver exceptional experiences by providing professional development to staff.

Students can share how they and their friends have learned to set time limits for themselves and insist that they participate in non-phone-related activities. Students also quickly point out that social media does not depict someone's day-to-day life. Social media posts highlight the best parts of the day or significant accomplishments. Very few posts discuss or share the challenges or failures that led to the posted success story. Lastly, students

FIGURE 2.4. Professional learning. *Source:* Susan Moore, August 24, 2022.

have learned what to share and where to share it. There are helpful hints, and when appropriately curated and guided, the voices of our students are exactly the professional learning from which our staff can most benefit as they navigate the benefits and challenges of social media in their classrooms.

Schools need to be proactive when dealing with social media-generated student issues. They can teach their students how to navigate the challenging world of social media by sharing real stories with them. Let current students know about reactions to controversial posts and how staff supported students in bringing issues to a successful conclusion. Use the school-based mentoring time to teach students appropriate social media etiquette and safety for the internet and social media.

Students need to know how to avoid and be aware of online predators and scams designed to exploit them. Students of all ages need to know the consequences of online teasing, being mean online, and online bullying. Students should be encouraged to ask for help from adults in their school when they feel guilty or threatened. Students can also benefit from learning strategies on how to determine the factualness of online material, as well as how to disconnect when needed. Adults also require professional learning around social media challenges. Provide school staff and families with training on social media safety, vocabulary, and student support.

Hashtags can be a good starting point for educators looking to connect, share, and learn. Educators also create their own educational resources by learning from books, podcasts, and blogs, not to mention the countless educators who moonlight as social media influencers sharing many creative practices. Educators can utilize various platforms to ensure learning and social media content is easy to locate, retrieve, share, and operate.

We are seeing more and more educators sharing their learning with colleagues across the country through numerous social media channels. Those serious about using social media for professional staff learning must recognize the unlimited information that social media can provide and limit hours and hours of scrolling through the vast network of resources. Refine your search, be open to others' ideas, and embrace new learning.

With limited professional development days built into a teacher's contract and numerous state and federal mandates and requirements soaking up many available allotted hours, school districts and teachers are exploring new professional learning options. These challenges have opened the door to social media use for teachers' professional learning and development. Teachers appreciate the choice and flexibility that social media and professional development provide them.

Many districts have been carving out regularly scheduled professional learning time for years for their staff. You may have heard the adage that some of the best professional development comes from the teacher down the hall. Imagine a world where the hallway is endless. A new professional learning community (PLC) for educators is taking hold through social media. Collaboration is a cornerstone of the education profession. The best teachers share open and honest feedback with their colleagues and open their doors so their peers can also support them. Today's top teachers also use social media to expand their professional learning networks with educators outside their school walls.

Social media allows access to on-demand, just-in-time, quick hits of professional learning. The busy teacher looking for ideas to implement in their classroom tomorrow can take to social media and search for ideas related to the curriculum unit and grade level to engage students and connect with real-life experiences and professionals in the field. Teachers can look for ways to engage parents, create a new bulletin board, find lesson plan templates, or seek suggestions for struggling students. There is no need to reinvent the wheel when so much innovation is at our fingertips.

For some teachers who teach unique subjects or singleton classes, social media may be the only way for them to connect with teachers who are instructing the same courses. Just like our students, teachers learn differently. Social media allows teachers to select videos and work with colleagues worldwide with similar instructional styles and learning needs. So tell your Calculus teacher—no need to fear; we can connect you with a colleague from another school, district, or state.

While social media garnered usage numbers for entertainment and personal social networking, educators are seeing the value of social media for professional learning. Educators connect with educators globally rather than simply visiting a successful teacher in their school, district, or state. With no direct costs and no set timelines for usage, social media will continue to expand its reach into educational professional learning. Teachers will continue to share best practices, collaborate, and reach out for assistance from educators they come to know from their professional social media networks.

Many educational professionals now have Twitter/X channels, Instagram accounts, Facebook pages, and TikTok content. Staff members can now get advice, tips, and tricks that can be applied in the classroom tomorrow from an expert today through their various social media channels. Encourage your staff to identify professionals in the field who have an active social media presence. Read the reviews and determine who can help your team feel comfortable and help your district succeed.

As you seek advice and direction from experts in your field, determine your specific need. For example, if you are looking for a math instructional technique, look to a colleague with great student engagement. If you are looking for a creative way to engage students with technology, find a teacher in your building who has received training and has successfully integrated technology into the classroom. Social media provides a vast network of experts for you to view and connect with virtually; choose the ones whose educational philosophy aligns best with your views and values.

Most education professional learning organizations and curriculum leaders have an active social media presence. Recommend vetted sites to your teachers and help them identify resources that align with your district's curricular goals. While Teachers Pay Teachers is a popular site for lesson plans and other resources, reviews of the material have questioned the quality of some of the resources. Continue to insist that your teachers remain the instructional experts and that central office professionals are involved in making curricular decisions with your teacher team.

Artificial intelligence may provide a better path for those looking to make their planning more efficient or their pedagogy more engaging and rigorous. With a few simple prompts, you can create rubrics, lesson plans, assessments, or exemplars. These can easily be simplified or scaled up for readability or even translated into other languages. Of course, like anything pulled from the Internet, it should be reviewed by a content expert before being distributed to students.

Ensure that your curriculum supervisors know what sites teachers use for materials and help them identify standards-aligned resources. Consider curating a list of professional learning social media pages for teachers to follow based on content area and grade level. Follow the vendors of your curriculum materials as they will offer webinars, resources, and strategies that can be implemented in your classrooms immediately. Most importantly, encourage your teachers to give it a try. After all, we learn from our failures and mistakes.

When teachers share their work on social media channels, they provide opportunities for others to learn from them and receive confirmation from their peers that their work is appreciated and valued. As school administrators face increasing demands for their time, we often lose sight of validating our staff's work. A quick like or thumbs-up on social media may be precisely what our educators need. As you implement social media into your professional learning plan, give your teachers a voice and choice.

Meeting our students where they are will require all our educators and parents to present materials in new and engaging ways. Our students want to be challenged and engaged, and their brains are used to absorbing lots of information at fast paces. Students love social media because of the stimulating, funny, engaging, and random content. The videos, hashtags, and simple likes are engaging features that connect with our students.

Social media has changed our lives in so many ways. The fact of the matter is that this is our new reality, whether this is a positive paradigm shift or not. One thing is sure: how we interact, socialize, and communicate has changed forever. Once we recognize these forthcoming changes, we can discuss what this means for our children and the educational institutions that serve them. We can begin planning for a successful implementation that recognizes there is a time and place for social media usage.

Technology integration has been a critical lever for improving many school systems. The Meriden Public Schools is one such example. While the Board of Education adopted more student-centered policies that enhance technology in the hands of our students and staff, they have also accepted our guiding principle, core values, and community-driven portrait of a graduate. Meriden Public Schools' guiding principle states, "all students must be able to access digital resources to expand their world. To accomplish this goal, students and staff must be provided with professional learning and development opportunities to purposefully and safely navigate the world of social media."

The district's core values are as follows: we all learn differently, voice and choice matter, learning spaces need to be flexible, and anytime, anywhere learning is enhanced and supported. Social media has supported different student learning styles and given our students a voice and choice. Social media can also be accessed in flexible learning spaces anytime and anywhere.

Through a foundation grant, Meriden Public Schools developed an authentic community-driven portrait of a graduate. This portrait identified the competencies our students need to be successful later in life. The portrait identified the following competencies: I am a learner, I am a thinker, I am an advocate, I am a collaborator, and I am prepared. Our students must continue learning about social media and consider what sites or venues support their goals

FIGURE 3.1. Meriden Public Schools guiding principle. *Source:* Photo created by Google Gemini. Image created by Meriden Public Schools, June 23, 2025.

and desires. Various social media platforms allow our students to advocate their positions and collaborate with others. Lastly, social media can help our students be prepared for their next journey in life, whether it be college, competitive employment, training programs, or the military.

How can we bring what we know about how students access information into the classroom to create more engaging learning experiences for all students? How schools connect with parents, students, and teachers is no longer a printed flyer in a backpack

FIGURE 3.2. Meriden Public Schools core values_1. *Source:* Photo created by Google Gemini. Image created by Meriden Public Schools, June 23, 2025.

FIGURE 3.3. Meriden Public Schools core values_2. *Source:* Photo created by Google Gemini. Image created by Meriden Public Schools, June 23, 2025.

or a traditional parent night at their child's school. Lately, all you hear about is how students are misusing social media. In addition to using social media for entertainment and social interaction, students use it to support their school and career ambitions. Students are maximizing social media's vast reach to meet their personal objectives, from finding information about colleges to securing internship opportunities to promoting their unique talents.

While school districts have highlighted their relevant concerns about social media's negative impact on student learning and mental health, students themselves have also used social media for academic assistance and their own social-emotional well-being. Social media platforms can improve student engagement, enhance a student's communication skills, create a safe place for student interaction, and encourage personalized student learning. Of course, students who spend too much time on social media may face productivity and time management challenges.

Students who enjoy social media are engaged and would be excited to incorporate it into their school day and learning experiences. You haven't seen engagement until you tell a room full of sophomore students that their Civics class will be initiating a social media campaign to support a cause that is important to them. Education officials must be honest with themselves, lawmakers, parents, and their home communities.

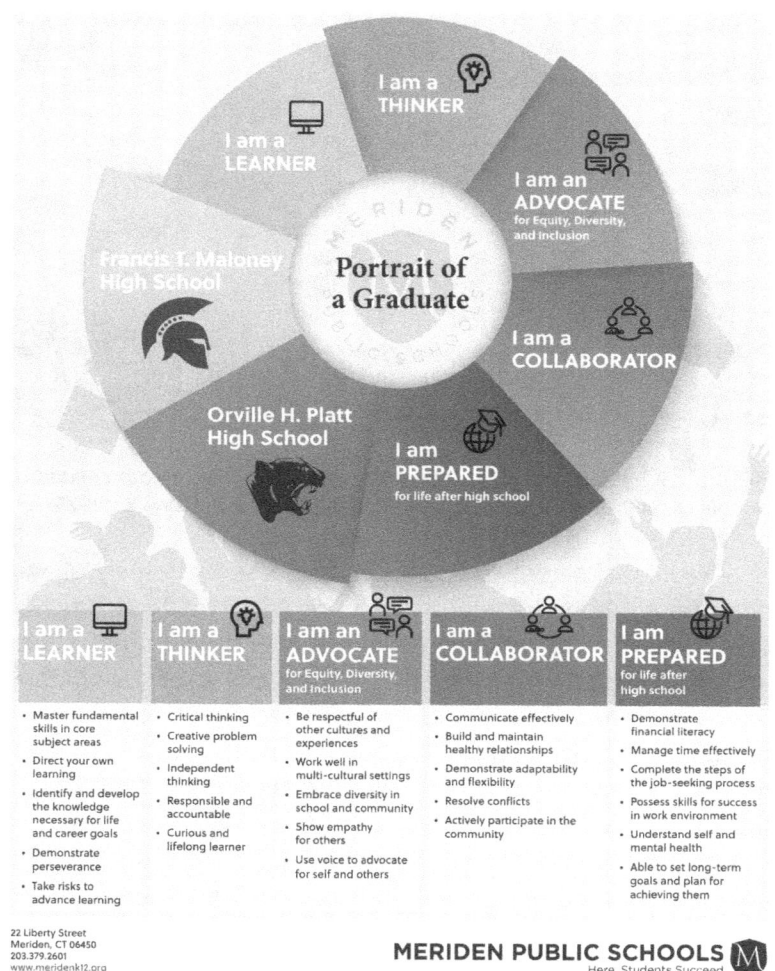

FIGURE 3.4. Meriden portrait of a graduate. *Source:* Meriden Public Schools.

Social media is a part of our students' daily routine, and it's time for our schools to meet them there. The days of reading the local newspaper are already being replaced with news feeds and social media posts.

The days of personal notes and written cards have also been replaced with text messages and social media posts. Visit any secondary school or college campus that has stood firm and avoided the misguided cell phone bans. You will see students of different ages and backgrounds engaged with their cell phones and the valuable connections and learning options these phones provide to them. Users need to maximize the benefits of technology while not letting it take over their entire social life.

Teacher lessons must be student-centered, personally engaging, and support student ownership over key learning tasks. Are our schools and teachers ready to let go and give students greater ownership and responsibility for their learning? Are our communities and political leaders supportive of the shift in teaching and learning? If the social media giants stop pushing algorithms, will our students be happier and more successful? We believe so! Students enjoy scrolling through videos on social media, swiping through friend requests, and providing thumbs up and hearts to posts they approve of and connect with daily. Are our classrooms designed to support these conversations? Have we trained our staff and students?

Our most creative, innovative teachers, and most well respected by their students, use social media to challenge and engage their learners. A simple online chat can engage students and help them learn from one another. We have also seen teachers hold debates with students on X with a specific hashtag for easy entry into the discussion and debate. Teachers use social media to engage their students, and we have also witnessed tech-savvy principals and superintendents using it to engage their parent community better.

Sharing school events and news, hosting virtual meetings, and reaching out for assistance with committee membership and fundraising efforts can be enhanced with the power of social media. Parents have supported schools' social media efforts as their busy schedules make social media a great way to stay connected with their children's school. Students and parents are looking to receive important school information in a timely, user-friendly manner.

Will this approach work for some of our most disengaged and disenfranchised students? It certainly can't hurt to try! Educators can organize group projects, share resources, gain insights from other educators on reaching struggling students, learn about various strategies for teaching specific content or units, and connect students to the larger community.

What about our high performers? Many high performers are motivated by grades, class rank, scholarships, awards, and college admission options. The most successful students typically excel with or without group work, catchy videos, or technologically rich lessons. Students learn better with an engaging curriculum and inspiring instruction, regardless of classes taken or past performances.

The pandemic made educational technology imperative for all schools, staff, and students. Today, there is no turning back. How do we assure our parents that the apps are safe and ensure our students are safe using them? We have seen district leaders ban social media platforms due to concerns about data privacy. There has to be a better way! So, we encourage school districts to educate their students and staff and leave the banning out of the equation.

While removing the apps from publicly funded devices is undoubtedly an option, it won't stop our students from using them. Students will hear the end of the school day bell and anxiously rush to access their cell phones and social media feeds. That is why we recommend educating your students and families about the pitfalls and healthy use guidelines. An honest approach is always best. Don't just share horror stories but also educational successes, high-quality learning experiences, and benefits gained from student exposure.

Check what apps are being used in your schools and classrooms. Ensure those apps do not present risks to your students, schools, and communities. Check to be sure they do not share students' personal information with third parties or expose students to digital ads. While these concerns are valid, they open up an opportunity to do what we do best: educate! It provides a reason to teach students how to navigate the world of social media safely and successfully.

Multiple educational professionals maintain social media sites that your teachers and administrators can use as sources of expertise and inspiration. Experts share strategies through podcasts, Twitter chats, and various video posts. Many curricular resources now include a digital component, and vendor partners provide valuable professional development opportunities to ensure that their products are leveraged to the fullest extent possible. Combining books and digital content can improve student engagement and learning outcomes.

When making a large investment in curriculum resources, do your research and see what others, including colleges, are posting about the product. When investing a substantial amount of money in a product, check out social media to see what others are saying about the learning tool. All vendors will share references supporting their product, but dig deeper and see what other direct users say about it. Follow your vendors and be sure to receive the latest product updates, enhancements, and supplemental products.

What do those who use the product every day say about it? Educators often share templates and strategies that will work in your classrooms. Those tips and tricks from colleagues may be invaluable and provide an action plan for successful implementation. Your colleagues across the country have often provided an endorsement or statement of concern. Surf through social media and get an honest answer to your questions. Reputable companies understand the importance of providing support to their school partners. Many have created social media pages and groups dedicated to supporting product use and allowing end users to ask questions and receive feedback from other users worldwide.

Educators may also find user support groups for specific products. For example, many vendors create support groups, which include training resources, lesson plan templates, and back-to-school resources. In addition to on-demand videos, home-school communication businesses hold virtual "summer camps" for their users. It is vital that educators not only understand how to teach using these digital tools but also help their students develop into good digital citizens.

Students will live and work in a technology-rich world that requires them to navigate social media at home and in the workplace. Social media will open up numerous business opportunities for some entrepreneurs. Who will be next to sell items made in their garages to a worldwide market? Our students must learn to be responsible, respectful, and safe in a new, wide-open learning and leisure virtual environment.

Our children and families are ready to reap the benefits of social media; are our educational institutions prepared to lead the charge? Students and parents are already connected to social media through Instagram, Snapchat, or X. Schools have always been the catalyst for change, where the playing field gets leveled and innovation flourishes. We cannot let the fear of the unknown derail us from embracing the power and prowess of social media channels.

Social media is not a distraction for our students; it is an attraction for them. So how can we make sure our teachers understand how to use it productively and that our students are responsible digital citizens? With a simple click, social media can connect students and teachers to others worldwide. Many schools use social media posts to communicate with parents and share pictures, school updates, and parent engagement opportunities.

So, how can social media be helpful in the classroom? Social media can effectively promote and share the great work of our students. It can also bring life to the concept of anytime, anywhere learning and be used as a communication tool to connect with students, staff, and parents. As we prepare students to be good digital citizens, social media can be used to share best practices and key considerations for online responsibility. Since about 2010, social media has changed our lives and gained worldwide popularity. So whether we like it or not, schools must educate students on effective usage.

Model the appropriate use of social media during classroom lessons. Students can learn to communicate in 280 characters or less, respond to a prompt with an image or short video, and simulate online interaction. In a safe, controlled learning environment, students can learn how to create engaging, appropriate posts. With a stack of Post-it notes, students can simulate online interactions. Most importantly, the activity should be connected to the content standards.

Provide students with a prompt, and ask them to post a reply. Classmates can like posts with a sticker and reply with a new Post-it note. As students develop their skills, the class can work in a closed online platform to post responses, including graphics, videos, and links. Given the proliferation of young adults torpedoing their careers, reputations, or both with ill-conceived social media posts, one could easily make the case that we have an obligation to coach responsible use.

Teachers can also discuss with students the benefits of expanding and accessing the additional resources and how it aids their learning. By connecting to their community and seeking opportunities for students to collaborate on projects outside of class, staff can prepare students for the opportunities the social media-savvy world presents. Experts can be made available to engage with your students and to answer questions about what they post. Following current events can keep your classroom engaging and provide real-world experiences for students.

So much of what students learn is through what they see, so our teachers must model these essential behaviors. Each action taken online and through social media becomes part of a student's digital footprint. Poor choices today can have lingering

Artificial Intelligence FAQs for Teachers and Administrators

Can I use AI as a teacher or administrator?
Yes! Most AI resources are open to staff on the district network.

Can students create accounts and access AI in school?
No. Currently, available AI content generators require end users to be 18 and up. However, this does not mean students are not using these apps at home. You can demonstrate how AI works in a class lesson, but please don't require students to use AI as part of an assignment.

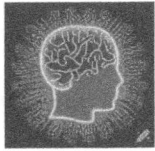

What do I need to know before using AI?
Writing an accurate prompt will help achieve the desired results. You can specify the length, style, and items to include. The better the prompt, the better the results.

AI Hallucinates and Confabulates - In other words, it makes stuff up. Always check results for accuracy.

AI may exhibit bias in its responses due to the data sets, algorithms, and human designers.

Where can I try AI?
Google Practice Sets in Google Classroom
https://bard.google.com/
https://chat.openai.com/auth/login
https://www.craiyon.com/
https://www.khanacademy.org/khan-labs

What if I suspect a student's assignment was generated using AI?
There are a number of tools listed below that can determine the probability that AI was used to generate a piece of work. Conferencing with students to determine their understanding of what they have submitted, comparing it to a student's handwritten work, and requiring multiple drafts of an assignment are other strategies.

Detect AI Generated Content
Google Originality Reports
https://gptzero.me/
https://contentatscale.ai/ai-content-detector/
https://openai-openai-detector--f4d78.hf.space/
https://writer.com/ai-content-detector/

Updated 8/20/2023

FIGURE 3.5. Artificial intelligence FAQs for teachers and administrators. *Source:* Meriden Public Schools.

consequences in the future. Digital tools continue to advance, and students need to learn to use these tools responsibly. The advent of artificial intelligence will change how we learn and work and must become part of the curriculum landscape.

As schools continue to wrestle with the need for greater student engagement, improved academic results, technology-savvy graduates, globally connected students, and mentally healthy adolescents, we must keep the cell phones in the hands of our students, embrace and leverage the positive aspects of AI, and encourage academic social media use as the benefits are numerous. Students enjoy and are better engaged in real-time communications. Other students may participate more freely and consistently in online discussions or ask for assistance anonymously at any time.

Resources that enhance the depth of student learning can be easily shared at any time of the day. Students will also learn how to use social media appropriately by participating in online discussions with their peers. In addition to the numerous student benefits of social media usage, it will keep our parents better informed and our teachers continually learning. Lastly, facing budget challenges, all districts search for cost-effective learning options, and social media provides a free alternative.

Instagram, Facebook, X, YouTube, LinkedIn, Pinterest, and blogs are all tools that teachers can easily use to engage their students and bring life to their classrooms. Blogs can be used to have students post and share what they learned in class. X can be used to have students determine the credibility of a host of statements. TikTok and Instagram can be used to have students post and share videos, pictures, and images. LinkedIn can be used to help students learn how to market themselves to future employers. All these social media platforms have benefits for our students, staff, and schools.

Social media has become a learning communication and marketing tool. All school systems, large or small, urban, suburban, or rural, need to communicate with their stakeholders and highlight their districts. These two reasons alone, and the fact that it is free, are why all school leaders must know about social media's many benefits and associated challenges. We had these same discussions in our own districts, and it became clear that the benefits certainly outweigh the risks.

This does not mean social media and artificial intelligence tools such as Gemini and ChatGPT are appropriate for all grade levels. Teachers must become familiar with student data privacy laws at the state and federal levels and review terms of use and privacy policies with their administration before introducing social media in the classroom. It may be more appropriate for students under thirteen to mimic social media tools without actually using them. This strategy will prepare students to engage appropriately in the social media world that is awaiting them in the near future.

For example, while students may be watching or creating TikTok videos at home, their Terms of Service state, "If you are under age 18, you may only use the services with the consent of your parent or legal guardian." However, we know students love short, entertaining videos and seeing themselves on screen. Using Chromebooks or iPads, students can create and submit videos to respond to an assessment or explain an assignment in under three minutes.

Students can also respond to writing prompts using an X-like 280-character maximum content assignment. These are the strategies that can be employed to safely prepare underage students to interact with a vast curriculum, personalized instruction, and individualized assessments. Rather than avoiding engaging content and innovative instruction, school systems need to embrace it.

The National Education Association released survey findings that blamed social media and cell phones for negatively impacting students' mental health, interpersonal skills, and learning. Leaders expressed concern that social media and device use are negatively impacting student mental health in schools. All students deserve a welcoming school environment where they feel challenged and supported.

While all education stakeholders agree on the need for positive school climates, opposing opinions remain on ensuring positive student learning environments. What is too often left out of the conversation is the parent's perspective. They are a critical component in setting a course for policy adoption. More than simple surveys are likely required. As new technology and laws emerge, educating parents is critical in eliciting their support and feedback.

Some believe a cell phone ban will keep students off social media and negate the negative consequences of social media usage. Others believe the negative implications are far more significant than any drawbacks from cell phones and social media sites. Technology proponents feel that if educational institutions don't teach students appropriate use, no one else will do it, leaving students vulnerable.

Communities must look at poor facility conditions, overcrowded classrooms, increased crime, lack of parent and community involvement and support, and overburdened and disrespected teachers and staff rather than solely focusing on social media and cell phones. Our top eight recommendations for parents to encourage their children to use technology positively in the classroom and at home are:

- Model the behavior—demonstrate responsible use of technology.
- Limit your use—especially during family mealtimes and activities.
- Engage in meaningful online activities that help students develop critical thinking skills so that they can understand bias or misinformation.
- Open communication and a supportive environment help your child feel comfortable discussing concerns.
- Encourage digital citizenship: teach respect, avoid cyberbullying, and share online privacy concerns.
- Encourage offline activities so there is a balance.
- Remind parents that you need their help at school—please don't text your student during the day—your child is "working."
- It is also essential to involve parents in understanding educational technology.

Our top seven suggestions for districts to increase parent engagement include the following:

- Share ways parents can be connected and engaged even if they cannot be physically at the school.
- District Notification Tools provide training and support for parents in multiple languages.

- Use communication tools such as ParentSquare to provide a uniform platform for two-way communication, sign off on permission slips, sign up for conferences, and secure online payments.
- Google Meet—hold meetings with parents via Meets, allowing greater flexibility. When necessary, coach the end user on how to turn on closed captioning, which can also serve to translate the conversation into their preferred language.
- Leverage your student information system, such as PowerSchool, and teach parents how to monitor students' assignments, absences, and grades.
- Work with local not-for-profit agencies to create learning opportunities such as Web Wednesdays—a partnership with the local senior center and our high school students, topics vary, and many seniors bring their devices and learn how to use social media apps to communicate with friends and family.
- Host events that allow students to share the technology with their parents. In celebration of Computer Science Education Week and the Hour of Code, families spend an evening programming Ozobots, experiencing Virtual Reality, and writing lines of code with their students.

Social media and cell phones did not create all of society's problems, but they can help solve many of them if used appropriately. The tools that are on a cell phone can genuinely enhance learning if used appropriately; there is a time and place for them in the classroom, but a straight-out ban takes away opportunities that can be used to enhance learning. Cell phones can be distracting; how do we teach students to use technology's power in their hands and use it appropriately? Before cell phones, passing notes between students provided a distraction that needed to be addressed by the teacher. We must teach students to use devices appropriately and ensure dynamic, engaging lessons happen in all classes.

Certain AI tools require cameras and sensors, which are not inherent in most Chromebooks but are built-in to the power of a cell phone. We once had similar discussions about calculators, laptops, and tablets. Should we ban smartwatches? Fitness trackers? At what age do we allow them? Schools are a safe

FIGURE 3.6. Hour of code. *Source:* Meriden Public Schools.

place to learn appropriate guidelines and behaviors. Educational institutions need to reinvent the teacher as a leader, including social media, cell phones, and AI.

Social media challenges and student mental health concerns must inform, but cannot stop our educational institutions from embracing technology, such as cell phones, artificial intelligence, and social media. Like the race to the moon, nations are racing to leverage artificial intelligence ahead of others. As AI continuously improves, nations sense the urgency to lead and control AI development and usage. AI has the potential to influence the world's economy, recreate jobs, advance scientific and medical research, and redefine how wars are fought.

While nations around the globe are doing all they can to build AI operations to support their citizens, here in America, we fear that cell phone bans and social media challenges might deter us from embracing the enormous power of AI. Just as we made sure we were the first to get a human on the moon, we must be sure that we are the ones to control AI. The United States has an advantage over the other nations that we must not lose.

American tech firms control the most powerful AI systems in the world and spend much more than others to continue to advance their operations. Presently, Nvidia in California is the key producer of the necessary AI chips, with other credible alternatives in play. To win this race, America must refrain from banning devices, avoid overregulation, and not ignore the need to educate its population, especially its students and their parents. Future employment opportunities will be available for individuals who understand AI and how it can positively impact work productivity.

Social media's reach and influence continue to expand, particularly with our children. TikTok, Snapchat, and Instagram are common apps that can be regularly found on our children's devices. This problem did not exist fifteen years ago, but how can we help our children navigate these apps safely and productively? First, we must ensure our students are of age, as no one under thirteen should use social media. Second, communicate with your child and monitor their usage of social media. Lastly, insist that your children are involved in outside activities where a cell phone has no place.

The tools on a cell phone can genuinely enhance learning if used appropriately. There is a time and place for them in the classroom, but a straight-out ban takes away opportunities that can be used to enhance learning and prepare students for the world that awaits them. So cell phones can be distracting; how do we teach students to use the technology's power in their hands appropriately?

Higher education institutions are resisting the urge and wave of political pressure to ban cell phones, abandon AI, and blame social media for all our problems. University reports tend to support technological advancements and integration in learning. These reports share the importance of building and supporting AI literacy and competency with students. College professors can create their own class policies and use AI to meet their course learning goals.

AI can generate false positives regarding student cheating, so assignments must be varied enough to ensure authentic student learning. For decades, we have evolved away from rote learning tasks to complex and creative work. This is the sort of work with which AI currently struggles. Coaching our teachers to develop tasks that are indeed authentic and complex not only supports learning but hinders students from looking for shortcuts through AI.

As higher education looks to support AI integration in their classrooms creatively, state leaders and staff members are left wondering what it will mean to them. Writing Centers have been a key component of student learning support on college campuses for over 100 years. Will AI replace them or change their roles? Or will these training centers become leaders in successful AI incorporation in students' educational and learning programs?

There is no doubt that AI provides numerous tools to help with the writing process. We believe AI provides an opportunity for writing centers to lead this new digital charge. The writing center staff can help students use AI tools purposefully and professionally to improve their written work and ensure students communicate clearly and effectively. We have already begun to see students and staff improve their written work with AI assistance.

We are excited about the power of AI! We are educating our administrators, BOE members, and non-certified staff on how AI can help them become more efficient in their jobs. We have been thrilled with the response of all our educational stakeholders. While many feel training is necessary, most recognize that AI is the future of our society and schools. All staff have access to AI tools—ChatGPT, Gemini, and Claude; many also use Grammarly and Canva, and both have AI integration.

High school students have access to AI in dual credit classes. Instructors encourage students to use AI to get differing opinions and then explain why they support their chosen responses. Mastery Projects can be used to evaluate AI responses and continue to improve student work. Middle School and High School classes piloted Sidekick AI Academy. This is an excellent space for students and teachers to learn how to use AI chatbots; it complies with student data privacy and allows teachers to review and provide student feedback on their interaction with the chatbot. Students did not interact with a Large Language Model (LLM) but smartly used AI tools with guardrails.

AI is here to stay! It may look different in the future, but we must teach students how to use the tool as they will be using bots in the workplace, and future employers will be looking for employees with AI experience. AI assistance can help with mental health support, engage and challenge students, reduce the workload for teachers, help better engage students, and keep them on their learning tasks. Most importantly, AI can excite our students about learning in today's world!

Educators and educational institutions use AI for the following tasks:

- Quickly gather facts for comparative research.
- Create content that is accessible for all learners—reading level, translation.
- Write songs for learning—favorite tune and add a topic.
- Provide different perspectives on a topic of study.
- Provide tutoring—teach parts of a cell, math facts.
- Generate highly interactive activities that are appropriate for specific grade levels.

No organization is better positioned to educate children, families, and communities on the benefits and cautions of social media, cell phones, and AI. Integrating cell phones into the educational landscape is a topic of much debate. There are potential benefits of allowing cell phone use in schools. We asked Gemini to list the educational benefits of cell phones in the classroom and received the following helpful guidance below:

Educational Benefits

- Access to Information: Cell phones can provide students instant access to information, making research and learning more efficient.
- Digital Learning Tools: Many educational apps and platforms are designed for cell phones, offering interactive learning experiences.
- Personalized Learning: Cell phones can cater to individual learning styles and paces, allowing customized education.

- Collaboration: Students can use cell phones to collaborate on projects, share ideas, and communicate effectively.
- Real-World Skills: Using cell phones in school prepares students for the digital age and develops essential technology skills.

Practical Benefits

- Emergency Communication: Cell phones can be a lifeline for contacting help.
- Parental Communication: Schools can use cell phones to communicate with parents promptly and efficiently.
- Organization: Students can use cell phones for calendars, reminders, and time management.
- Accessibility: For students with disabilities, cell phones can provide assistive technology and support. For students who speak a language other than English, cell phones can allow them to quickly and easily understand and connect to content, teachers, and peers.
- It is important to note that while cell phones offer potential benefits, their use in schools must be carefully managed to prevent distractions and misuse. Implementing clear policies and guidelines is crucial. Cell phones, AI, and social media convergence have created a robust ecosystem that shapes our daily lives. Their roles are interconnected:

Cell phones are the platform:

- Accessibility: Cell phones provide easy access to the Internet, making social media platforms always available.
- Portability: Users can engage with social media on the go, supporting regular connectivity.
- Personalization: Through apps and customization options, cell phones personalize social media experiences to individual user preferences.

AI is the powerhouse:

- Personalization: AI algorithms analyze user behavior to deliver tailored content, ads, and recommendations.
- Content Creation: AI-powered tools generate text, images, and videos, automating the content creation process.
- Content Moderation: AI helps identify and remove harmful content, ensuring a safer online environment.
- User Experience: AI enhances user interactions through features like chatbots, virtual assistants, and augmented reality.

Social media is the arena:

- Content Sharing: Cell phones facilitate the creation and sharing of content based on AI recommendations.
- Community Building: Social media platforms build connections and communities supported by AI-powered interactions.
- Marketing and Advertising: AI optimizes ad targeting and delivery, maximizing ad reach and consumer engagement.
- Data Collection: Social media platforms gather vast amounts of user data, which AI analyzes to inform decisions and recommend improvements.

Cell phones provide the platform, AI powers the intelligence, and social media serves as the stage for these elements to interact and influence our digital lives. Educators and educational institutions have always looked ahead, planned for the future, and prepared students for careers that did not even exist yet. While it may be a decade or longer away, AI will provide medical assistance to change and cure numerous health constraints. There is already discussion about how maintaining brain waves for cognitive functioning might lead to early detection of dementia.

Let's ensure that our schools see the value of the cell phone for learning, the power of AI for information, and the reach of social media to communicate and connect with others. Share appropriate use of guardrails with students and staff, but insist that our schools continue to be innovation leaders. Just as we have created STEM Labs, Genius Labs, Advanced Placement Lounges, and Multilingual Lounges to advance and enhance student learning, we must be courageous in our efforts to engage and educate our learners through the powerful use of our cell phones, AI, and social media. If education systems are not, then who will ensure that our students successfully navigate the world of social media?

Multiple books on leadership strategies encourage us to remember to take the time to celebrate success. Social media platforms not only provide an opportunity to celebrate success and district achievements but also serve as a vehicle to share it with a broad audience. Students need more opportunities for engagement than 6 hours a day, 180 days a year. Extracurricular activities and technology can expand the school experience and help create a positive school climate and culture that makes a difference for students, staff, and parents.

Schools are often the centerpiece of their students' lives, where extracurricular activities, sports, arts and music programs, and school and community events happen regularly. Celebrating success and achievement through social media means building excitement for the first day of school, the pep rally, or attendance at school events, community pride when recognizing diverse stakeholders, and celebrating a wide range of cultural events.

Creating a positive climate and culture requires educators to share and celebrate success in many forms. Districts that value climate and culture have unique ways to celebrate their students and staff. Monthly student awards are given to worthy "Model Citizen" students at Board of Education meetings. Yearly student leadership awards are shared and presented by the superintendent and Board of Education. Teachers are acknowledged when their students perform well on standardized testing measures.

National Blue Ribbon School signage and State Schools of Distinction banners are prominently displayed on school buildings and hallway walls. Performer Awards/ Ribbons are given to any teacher whose students perform 5 percent better than the state average for the percent target achieved on mandated Smarter Balanced Assessments. These awards/ribbons are proudly displayed in classrooms across the district and shared through our social media platforms.

What a great day for the neighborhood elementary school, which received word that it would receive the nation's most prestigious honor, the National Blue Ribbon Award. As the principal and assistant principal sat in their office conference room with great pride and enthusiasm, they thought about how best to get this great news out to students, staff, families, and the community. Who should receive notification first? Does the Central Office

FIGURE 4.1. Sports highlights. *Source:* Panther Football, October 25, 2024.

want to alert the Board of Education before any official school notification? Will the news media air the story?

With only three schools in the state receiving this special recognition, there was a strong likelihood that the state media network would share the schools' success stories. The school leadership team sprang into action. First, they let the superintendent email the Board of Education before school notifications. Second, they alerted their staff with congratulations and appreciation. Third, they used the home-school communication system to inform their families about this great honor. Then, they had a schoolwide assembly to honor its students who led the school to this prestigious honor.

While thanking the staff and students, with music in the background, pictures and videos were taken by numerous staff members in the building. These pictures and posts made it on social media in a matter of moments. With numerous likes coming in, the video and picture posts from the school began being shared by families and community members. The social media frenzy led to local and statewide media coverage. TV networks were on-site, and the positive school climate and culture were on full display. Social media shared the incredible news and provided a visual for the school, staff, and students to view.

The Board of Education also offers a monthly Community Support Award to community partners and businesses that give back to the school system and make a difference for students. There is no denying that student, staff, and community award winners appreciate these awards, but more importantly, they feel valued and respected. However, the district is the real winner when these positive success stories are shared across the district and community through social media channels.

With a commitment to this philosophy and diverse programs in place, who will ensure they successfully launch? No matter what state you live in, whether you have a local media outlet or not, you can share positive social media stories about your students and recent graduates. This will show that your students are safe and thriving and build the community's confidence in their schools. That is why schools must maximize the power of social media to share their story.

Schools that tell their story have better chances of getting their latest referendum for school projects approved. Private schools use social media to connect with alumni and increase their fundraising efforts. As the demand for teachers and support staff continues to rise, school districts use social media to recruit and retain staff. Districts facing competition from private schools, charters, and magnets are using social media to keep their enrollment numbers up and retain enrollment.

Will we rely on intercom announcements and hardcopy newsletters? Will we use our parent notification systems? Or will we meet our students and parents where they are on social media platforms? Some schools are creating their own YouTube videos to increase awareness and participation. While we see great value in face-to-face communications and a personal approach, we also support a multifaceted approach that includes appropriate social media outreach to students and families.

Building a positive climate and culture for your school district can be enhanced through social media. Progressive school districts are tweeting new hires, staff award recipients, and student successes. Social media is very visual and is a great way to engage

FIGURE 4.2. Teacher appreciation week. *Source:* Cheshire Public Schools, May 6, 2024.

your school community, including your staff. Districts use social media campaigns to build their brand and develop credibility with their consumers, students, and families. Many districts have launched staff spotlights, team member highlights, and other ways to recognize, promote, and share their team members' successes.

Social media can help you start a cost-free way of recognizing your employees with a favorable, regular ad content program. Employees have shared that they enjoy being recognized for their performance, value, and teamwork. Social media and its positive ad videos allow schools and districts to put a face and a smile on their story. This approach attracts an audience, enables people to relate, and, when done most effectively, inspires them to take action. Now that you have the perfect picture or video, it's time to create an engaging caption that will have people stop to read, quote, like, and comment on your amazing students and staff.

So, you're ready to launch a social media strategy for your school district. As you plan with your team, be clear about your intended audience. Once you define your audience, you must select the right platform to connect with your intended viewers. Educators may use social media platforms to reach students, staff, and parents. While students may be reached best by Instagram, parents may be best reached through Facebook.

Five commonly used social media platforms in school districts are Facebook, Instagram, X, LinkedIn, and Pinterest. All five options can benefit and support a school district's communication plan and engagement efforts. Facebook is the most extensive social media platform, and school districts commonly use it to connect with parents. Facebook provides a platform to share videos, photos, events, and job opportunities.

Instagram is an excellent platform for communicating with students. Instagram provides an engaging platform to connect with students. It provides a platform that uses designs to share pictures and videos. X is another platform that school districts commonly use to engage with their stakeholders. When posting messages, character restrictions ensure brief, direct messages that include creative hashtags. These hashtags are quick attention grabbers that help ensure your content is seen and read.

School districts use LinkedIn to recruit staff members. LinkedIn posts should be about job openings, staff success stories, and anything that highlights the district's benefits to its students. A newer addition to school district social media campaigns is Pinterest. Pinterest provides a vehicle to post pictures that share how your school district is being creative, innovative, and enjoyed by students, staff, and families.

Districts that have led the charge into practical social media usage have a few things in common. First, they talk with their students. Finding out what students want for information and where they would be sure to see it is an excellent start for any district launching social media efforts. Advanced social media districts have students create and distribute social media content.

Just as schools use teachers to lead digital transformations, students can help lead social media efforts.

In one district, teachers receive "I'm Charged" status by demonstrating their technology skills and opening their classrooms to their peers. Staff appreciate the opportunity to learn from their esteemed colleagues rather than a self-proclaimed outside expert. Districts can launch a similar social media program for student leaders who demonstrate their social media savvy. This can be done safely and cost-effectively in any school district.

Now that you have a team of teachers and students ready to launch and lead your social media campaign, it is time to provide them with training to ensure they are designing engaging content and have a local plan for posting timelines. Schools will also need to ensure they are appropriately achieving their social media goals in accordance with state laws, board policies, district guidelines, and community expectations.

Today's fast-paced culture requires schools and districts to ensure information is readily accessible, quickly delivered, and

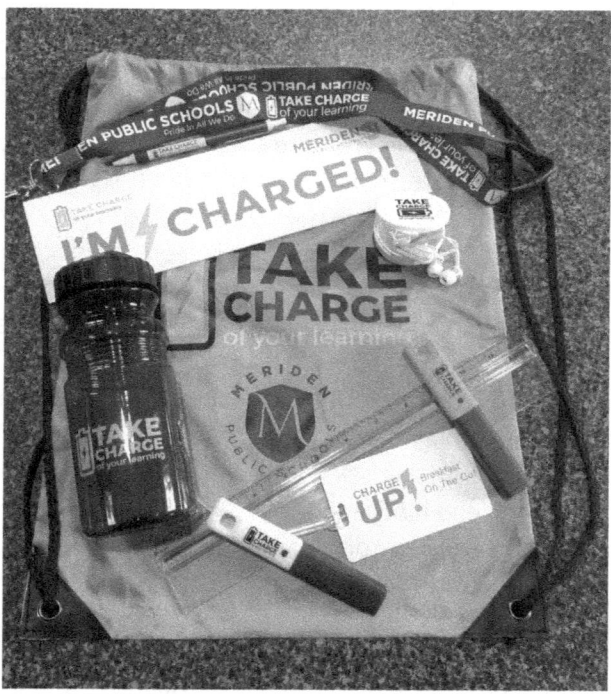

FIGURE 4.3. I'm Charged. *Source:* Meriden Public Schools.

read by the intended audience. That is why messages must grab someone's attention and share critical information first. Grammar and spelling must be accurate, but emojis and tagging are helpful ways to ensure your message gets to the intended audience and that it is read. Also, if you have urgent messages that must be read immediately by parents or staff, your communication plan needs safety considerations built in. Direct messaging to parents and guardians, in addition to social media postings, might be required.

We continue to see more and more public schools use social media channels to create their brand, communicate with their stakeholders, and share information with the greater community. Private schools have used social media to increase their customers and highlight the desirable features of their schools. Public schools looking to keep up should utilize social media accounts, clarify their stakeholders, design and create engaging digital content, and post on school and district social media channels.

One superintendent turned to social media to share his post-pandemic strategies to foster a positive school climate. He posted videos on Facebook, Instagram, and X. He shared a day as a preschooler, a participant in school musicals, and racing on field day. The superintendent received an overwhelmingly positive response and has seen increased job applications for open positions and greater trust among families. All district leaders need to make this happen is a cell phone and the courage to open their schools up to the community.

The Lockdown

It was just another early March morning as everyone—students and staff alike—began the countdown to April vacation. The stretch from New Year's to February break always comes at the right time. However, all educators know the February, March, and April stretch can be trying. So, here we are at the end of March, less than two weeks from vacation, when one of our two high schools went into lockdown.

The school resource officer attempted to support a school staff who effectively and quickly intervened to derail a group fight.

The school resource officer called for backup as tempers rose and threats grew louder. The situation indeed could have spiraled out of control; what was really out of control was all the misinformation on social media. Before school staff and police officials handled the situation, they were forced to deal with misinformation that caused fear.

Despite reposts of weapons, assaulted teachers, and student injuries, that was not the case at all. These false reports put fear in students, staff, and families and had police racing to the high school from across the city. Some pushing and shoving did occur; the inaccurate misinformation on social media posts caused more issues than the actual incident that occurred. So, how did the school respond?

The school shared a factual statement with the media, sent out a parent, student, and staff notification email and text, and used social media to report factual information. Clarifying the record and ensuring all stakeholders received a consistent message was necessary. The school also benefited from the community reposting the official statement on their personal social media channels. However, the negative impact was felt by all, and the school climate suffered from it.

Of Concern

Not everyone believes social media can have a positive impact on education. The American Federation of Teachers (AFT) represents the second most teachers in the country. The AFT is concerned that social media is negatively impacting a teacher's ability to engage students and student mental health. Fears surround students navigating an unregulated environment in the classroom and at home. Technology advocates, business executives, and many students disagree and believe social media can enhance teaching and learning.

Rather than suing social media companies, school systems would be better positioned to partner with them. Not only do our parents expect us to meet and inform them through social media, but so do our students. Let's not just say students' voices matter;

let's include them and encourage them to lead the discussions in social media chat rooms. Our students are comfortable navigating social media for information, collaboration, and support.

As the number of teens experiencing depression has drastically increased, we are all left to examine social media's role in this troubling situation. Are our teens abandoning part-time employment, extracurricular school experiences, community service opportunities, and other community-based sports, arts, and music options to spend more time on their cell phones? Or are our students searching for creative experiences that incorporate technology into their learning?

More importantly, what is the impact on mental health and well-being? Some states have shown an increase in teen depression and feelings of hopelessness that correlate directly with the use of social media. How will we get students away from their screens and back into organized, structured activities with their peers? There are differing opinions and contradictory research as to whether technology use is to blame for the mental health crisis facing our nation. What is clear is that technological advances are outpacing our schools' ability to navigate this new world successfully.

Many school districts do not have specific social media policies, and current technology policies do not even reference social media. Another concern with district technology policies is that they reference the importance of technology to learning but then discuss banning it from students who misuse their devices. Many policies mention the need for educating students about safe usage, but they do not specifically address mental health concerns.

None of these concerns should surprise us, as we have all witnessed the rapid pace of technological innovation and how AI and social media have impacted schools nationwide.

School districts should protect themselves by updating their policies to address social media usage in schools and ensure that new policies contain information on how they will provide education on the safe use of social media to students and staff.

These recommendations can be helpful to school districts looking to update their social media policies. Mental health must not be viewed as a social media issue or an isolated item for schools to address. We need a comprehensive approach that brings external support. If we are serious about addressing the health and welfare of our children, we must start with family support, community outreach, and school collaboration. Smart social media policies are good places for schools to start.

One state makes it illegal for minors' social media accounts to be influenced by algorithms that determine one's social media feeds. These algorithms drive content of interest, thus increasing the potential to become addictive to users, especially our children. The law also proposes banning notifications between 12:00 a.m. and 6:00 a.m. throughout the year and between 8:00 a.m. and 3:00 p.m. when school is in session.

Whether the state laws will go into full effect in the coming years remains as much of a mystery as whether social media providers will comply with parental consent and other requirements. With bipartisan support, we can expect to see more and more states adopt social media laws. We can also expect to see more and more lawsuits protecting First Amendment rights. Most importantly, schools must have a plan to educate their students, staff, and parents about the benefits and challenges of social media.

The U.S. Surgeon General and forty-two State Attorney Generals have asked social media platforms to provide health warning labels; however, the research connecting mental health care to social media remains inconclusive and limited. More concerning is that many leaders need to pay greater attention to the questions that social media brings to users. Students have shared that they have used social media to create peer networks, learn new activities, connect with relatives worldwide, study for their classes, and share encouraging videos and messages with others.

Some social networks are making changes to make their platform safer for younger users. Instagram sends anyone under eighteen, whether new to the platform or existing users, to their teen accounts. Their teen accounts will be private and restrict what content can be accessed by teen users. These changes are long overdue and have been embraced due to all the pending lawsuits. So what will these changes actually do?

Teens would have to accept who can follow them and see their accounts. Teens will also only be able to receive messages from people they follow or to whom they are already connected. There will also be a true mandated sleep mode when on the website platform for too long. While most groups applauded these changes, some, like the National Parents Union, want even more restrictions. We are still hopeful we can find that healthy balance that protects our children while advancing the power of technology.

While there is no debate that we have a national mental health crisis, the discussion about social media's role in the problem remains heated. Many articles state that they believe social media is a major contributor to the mental health crisis. Some studies have revealed that adolescents who check social media regularly become more impacted by the feedback that they receive on social media channels.

While other experts may disagree, there is no argument that social media has become a way of life for Generation Z. Some reports reveal that 95 percent of middle and high school students use social media. How can we teach adolescents to have a healthy balance? First, school districts must be aware of the mental health crisis and how it can impact their students and staff. Second, teach students to ask themselves the What, Why, Who, and Where questions: What am I posting? Why am I posting it? Whom am I posting it for? Where am I posting it? A simple way to look at any social media post is to ask yourself, "What would my mom say? What would my best friend say? What if my post was read on the school announcements?"

In our November 2022 School Administrator article, "Social Media: Friend or Foe?" we touch upon the intensifying questions about the mental health toll that cell phone use may be causing students all over the nation. In reviewing data from our safety management online provider, we saw over a 600 percent increase in suicide references and an overall 700 percent increase in violence references. These data cannot be ignored! Did social media use contribute to the alarming data? Either way, social media can increase awareness and offer our students and staff immediate support.

Seattle Public Schools was one of the first school districts to sue major social media companies over the mental health concerns of their students. While other districts have joined the legal battle, many experts believe the lawsuit will fail in the courts. However, the cases are gaining the public's and the press's attention and creating a platform to share how social media companies are marketing their highly addictive apps to students with no regard for mental health fallout. We must find common ground and put our students first.

Professors and lawyers have differing opinions on social media lawsuits. Supporters of the suit feel that social media companies must take responsibility, and communities must demand accountability. Others think the lawsuit is an overreach and will be a tough sell. These opponents of the lawsuit believe that social media companies are being unfairly blamed for the mental health crisis. They believe a large part of the problem lies with the parents and the lack of parenting.

Regardless of the outcomes of the more than a dozen lawsuits filed, the reality remains that, once again, our underfunded, under-resourced, understaffed schools are left to deal with this issue while still trying to climb their way back academically from the pandemic. Also, schools are dealing with social media challenges and mental health emergencies created by social media posts. Many of these schools have depleted support staff, and the teacher shortages have been severely felt in social work, psychology, and school counseling positions.

These were the first positions to be cut for years when budget reductions were necessary. Even with funding, districts are fighting for a limited qualified and certified applicant pool. Exacerbating the problem is the shortage of outside therapists for families who recognize the problem and require support. Most schools have experienced serious cyberbullying incidents related to social media, and many of these schools had difficulty getting social media companies to take them down. Recently, many schools nationwide have had to deal with threats that keep students home.

If schools are asked to do more, they must have the human and fiscal resources to keep students safe. All social media companies note that they prioritize teen safety and have tools to protect their users. Together, let's protect our students. TikTok published age restrictions and parental controls. YouTube noted Family Link as a way to support parents with their supervision efforts. Meta, too, stressed the ability of parents to limit screen time. Snapchat indicated that it uses human moderation to see problems before it sees a large audience. With social media here to stay and schools caught in the middle between companies and parents, the need for further research and discussion remains a top priority.

As schools try to use social media to engage and inspire students safely, social media companies are battling lawsuits, pointing out the parents' role in usage, and leaving schools to adjust to a new norm with limited resources and expertise. Schools are rightly concerned that students should not be subjected to questionable advertisements and that their information should not be shared with third parties. That is why districts should limit apps and require disclosures from any business partner.

Other experts wonder if limiting teen access to social media might create more problems than it attempts to solve. Rather than spending time and money on lawsuits, these resources could be invested in educational programs in media literacy. While some blame social media for the mental health crisis, others believe that social media is being made the scapegoat for our nation's rise in adolescent anxiety and depression. As schools ban cell phones, avoid and restrict AI, and blame social media for student mental health issues, we worry that we could be unintentionally harming our most vulnerable students who rely on social media for connection, comfort, safety, and health.

When schools create action plans to incorporate social media and technology use successfully, they can avoid the knee-jerk reaction to ban and limit. Instead, they can focus on educating all learners and supporting our most marginalized students as well. Many students' connection to information on the World Wide Web rests on their cell phones. Not all districts provide devices to students, and banning the technology that students may already have at their disposal will create an even more uneven playing field.

How can we maintain this focus and support all students? Below are some suggestions to get you started:

- Encourage school leaders to post a weekly highlight reel, identify a bright spot, or shout out a specific student, staff member, or grade level. What are some positive things that happened in the school this week? Remember to keep track of what is included to ensure an unbiased representation of students and staff.
- Promote an upcoming special event, then follow up with pictures or critical topics from the event itself. This may be

an art show, musical or theater performance, STEM night, or another school-based event.
- Participate in national social media campaigns like the ACT Center for Equity in Learning's American College Application Campaign (#WhyApply, #IApplied, #Accepted) or All4Ed Digital Learning Day (#DLDay).
- Work with your Athletic Director and coaches to feature athletes' accomplishments on and off the field.
- Profile your district's distinguished alumni, demonstrating that the foundation they gained while in your school system helped lead them to success.

As you begin your social media journey, we recommend defining your target audience. Whom do you want to reach, and with what information? Second, create clear, attainable goals. How often will you post, and what percentage of your stakeholders do you want to reach? Third, design authentic, personalized content. What you create and the quality of pictures and videos matter. Will you utilize your staff and students in the productions? Lastly, evaluate your campaign's performance and share results. Open, honest communication with your stakeholders and community is essential. Your new social media community must be able to trust you and see that social media channels are a vehicle to get accurate information.

Every day, you hear another story about how a school deals with the challenges created by social media posts. Sometimes, it comes from within, such as a current student or staff member posting something that violates district guidelines and policies. These social media challenges often arise from external players who need more connection to our schools or students. Schools will continue to deal with social media posts about school threats, ineffective leadership, troubling staff, poor transportation, coaching and sports issues, and just about anything that one can imagine—even crime in the community.

How can school districts use social media as a lever to improve school climate and culture? Educational institutions can use social media channels to share your district's goals, vision, and mission. Social media is a great platform to highlight successes as well as express appreciation to your students, staff, and community. Read

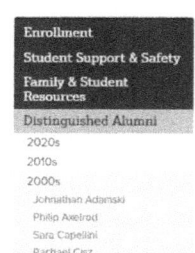

FIGURE 4.4. Distinguished alumni. *Source*: Meriden Public Schools.

student, staff, and school conversations, and get to know your players, but do not focus your energy on negative posts. Don't let negativity derail you from using social media's reach to build upon the positives of your school climate and culture.

Be sure to listen and learn from key stakeholders. Social media can give you honest data about how your students, staff, parents, and community feel about your schools. Have a clear campaign vision and choose whom in your organization will post to social media. Don't expect your social media launch to go perfectly, but don't let the fear of negative posts prevent you from using social media to create your brand, share your vision, and highlight your successes.

The platforms will continue to change, and the reach of social media will continue to expand and gain greater influence. Do you have your school district poised to meet this new paradigm? How will you use social media to recruit and retain talent, positively impact curriculum and instruction, build a positive climate and culture, and support systems for our operational needs and facility enhancements?

As the cost of educating our students continues to rise and budgets shrink, the need for districts to innovate becomes increasingly essential. Leveraging social media to identify grant opportunities and highlight a district's success can lead to funding for programs and initiatives that would otherwise fall victim to the budget ax. In no other venue could you immediately connect with so many constituents. For better or worse, social media immediately connects the planet, let alone your community. Educational leaders need to leverage that power to tell their stories and connect the community to their mission. This book is intended to provide the keys that unlock that proverbial door.

This chapter is designed to focus on the operational side of leadership. There are a myriad of applications for social media that extend into operations. District communications can significantly influence facilities investments, operational budgets, and human services, to name a few. At its core, social media is about sharing information. Regardless of the topic that you are posting about, you are influencing the mindset of the viewer. You may be communicating information during an emergency or posting about an impending budget meeting, but if you are not doing so conscious of the opportunity to positively shape the perspective of your schools, you are missing the mark.

It isn't a leap for any seasoned building or district administrator to imagine the following scenario. It is 3 p.m. on a school day, and the phone rings. The local television station is asking for comments about the bomb scare at your high school. Facebook is full of posts about it, complete with pictures of the two fire trucks, three police cars, and an ambulance at the building. The person who initiated the post "heard" about the threat from a friend. The reality is that the district was conducting a comprehensive security drill after school today. The following two hours will be spent diffusing the inferred and now proverbial bomb.

At first glance, educational leaders may dismiss the connection between social media and operations. We are so focused on instructional leadership that considering utilizing media for operations may be an afterthought. It would also be selling the value of such efforts short. We can't take for granted that educating stakeholders on all elements of our work is vital to any central office leader's social media strategy. The pictures and words shared in posts should be focused on bringing the community closer to the district's mission.

A well-informed stakeholder is more knowledgeable and can better advocate for the district. Even if your message recipient is not actively advocating, informed stakeholders are granted the knowledge and confidence to debunk misinformation. In an era of rampant misinformation, defeating inaccurate information may be even more critical to the health and prosperity of your school district than advocacy. Consider how your educated community could have quickly mitigated the misinformation surrounding the high school "bomb threat" post scenario.

Understandably, district leaders are most often focused on communicating with those stakeholders with whom we already have a direct connection: teachers, parents, staff, and students. While operations and capital investment issues are essential to this audience, these issues could benefit from a broader communications strategy. In some communities, capital improvement projects are voted on by the entire community. In other communities, these decisions are made by a group of elected officials.

Skilled district leaders employ social media messages to effectively educate and empower their community beyond the

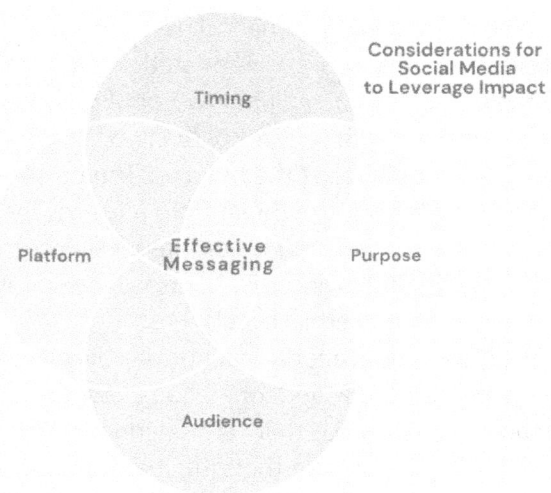

FIGURE 5.1. Considerations for social media to leverage impact. *Source:* Cheshire Public Schools.

classroom and into operations and facilities. Timing, purpose, platform, audience, and amplification are the key variables to consider in that messaging. Like much of what we deal with in leadership, these elements are not mutually exclusive and must be considered in concert to achieve the most effective results. Targeting your communications to your audience where they engage is critical to educate and inform the community.

Timing Considerations

In the scenario mentioned earlier, posts about the impending drill a week, three days before, and on the morning of the drill could have made an enormous difference. On occasion, things arise that require an immediate response. Not all events can be choreographed, but most can. Education and the events that occur over the course of a year are fairly predictable.

I first became a Cheshire Public Schools' administrator in 2005. I was hired as a middle school assistant principal. With all due respect to every principal I have ever worked with, my principal at the time, Don Wailonis, was the best I have ever seen. Among the hundreds of valuable lessons he taught me in our time together was that education is cyclical. The same general activities occur at the same general time every year. In the life of a principal, you know the open house will happen each fall. The winter concert is every December, and the promotion is in June. Along the journey of a school year, there are many predictable milestones.

Don kept a meticulous "tickler file" that he would label by month. He would dutifully remove the memos and notes from the previous year each month. What made this process so valuable wasn't the simple reminders but the constant improvement. Each memo or note was an assessment of the impact from the previous year. Notes would be recorded to highlight where communication wasn't clear or what updates were needed to improve the event.

Whenever we were engaged in an activity, we thought about what could improve it for the future. Sometimes, it was something big like bringing students to the open house next year so that they could act as tour guides. Often, it was something small like remembering to get plants to spruce up the podium for a presentation. On every occasion, though, we knew what had to happen the next time this event came around on the calendar.

Operations have a life cycle in the course of each year. Inevitably, you are pitching your budget, engaging in facility improvement efforts, or initiating hiring at the same time each year. Social media is used to enhance these efforts and educate a broader audience. The point is that each effort is a learning opportunity to improve your communications and operational outcomes year over year. Are you conscious of these opportunities and taking advantage of them?

Today, some companies provide social media posting calendars to districts. Call it a contemporary tickler file. If you posted about an upcoming event, how did it go? Was your post engaged well (with likes and comments)? Did you post enough before the event? A savvy administrator records improvements to make adjustments in the following year.

The timing of your social media post is an important factor for engagement. Whether it is a recruiting fair or budget meeting, you want people to be there and well informed. Sometimes, a duplicate of the post before the week of the event is adequate, but modifying the post to make it engaging in a different way gains attention. In my experience, nothing gains more engagement than including your students in the post!

If your initial post had music but no motion, consider adding a video, for example. While timing is important, it is also the most straightforward consideration in posting. Timing is only a matter of preparation. I have gone to a hybrid digital "tickler file" and my old-school paper file where I can make notes and plan future communications and practices.

Purpose Considerations

Covid-19 presented incomprehensible health and educational challenges for school systems. With health data changing rapidly, schools were in constant connection with their students, staff, and families. Schools sent home numerous messages and, at times, videos for stakeholders to view. While many of these messages were sent by school officials via their student and family engagement provider or posted on the official district website, numerous messages and videos were posted and recorded on social media sites.

Lesson one: You can be thoughtful about helping others get the word out for you. Districts can send their messages out only through their professional channels with the knowledge that someone will post them on social media for them. Lesson two: Whatever you share, others can grab and share a post. So keep that in mind and use it to your advantage. Get your word out there by leveraging the social media following of other people in your network.

All social media is used with a purpose. The purpose is more than the information you share. What do you want the viewer to take away from your post? Your audience should know about an upcoming event. However, don't assume your audience knows you want them to attend the event. If you post it as a call to action, tell the audience what you want them to do. "Please visit our tent at this weekend's festival! We will be there from 10 am-4 pm on Saturday." This sounds much different than simply posting the date and time. If the purpose of your post is a call to action, tell people what the desired action is.

I appreciate that superintendents have to be politically savvy and can't always be so direct as to say their goal is to get support to prevent proposed budget cuts. "Bring out your pitchforks and torches for tonight's budget meeting to fix these budget cuts!" is probably not the post you want to go with. Obviously, you need to use judgment and discretion when soliciting stakeholder involvement.

Nevertheless, careful consideration of the purpose of your communication is critical in engaging stakeholders. Failure to consider the purpose of your communication and the nuance within that post (both in words and images) can quickly land you on the wrong end of those pitchforks! Social media messaging requires even deeper scrutiny than verbal communication because there is limited context, and it is memorialized forever on the web. Think about your purpose when sending it.

Platform and Audience Considerations

According to Demandsage.com, there are approximately five billion social media users worldwide! The global population is only about eight billion. Facebook, WhatsApp, YouTube, Instagram, WeChat, and TikTok have over one billion subscribers. What you post on social media has massive global potential. Of course, most district leaders are attempting to avoid going viral globally. You are trying to target a specific group with your message. That is where knowledge of your purpose, the various social media platforms, and the demographics those platforms cater to is necessary.

Facebook (Meta) is America's largest social media platform, with nearly three billion monthly users. Nearly 30 percent of all users are between twenty-five and thirty-four years of age and spend about thirty minutes daily on the site. While Instagram users spend roughly the same amount of time on the platform, 30 percent of their users are between the ages of eighteen and twenty-four. There has been a clear shift from text-rich media to image and video-based media. According to Intelligence.com, the average American adult spent more than forty-five minutes daily on TikTok and another forty-five minutes on YouTube. That same source indicated that those same adults spent more than thirty minutes daily on Snapchat, Facebook, and Twitter/X each. That sounds bad enough, but consider that these data were from 2022 and are likely higher today.

Communications around district operations will vary by platform based on the timing, purpose, and audience you are targeting. Posting on various media ensures the greatest likelihood of reaching the broadest audience, but it can also be the most time-consuming. Data tell us that different platforms resonate with diverse audiences. In the same way, it is hard to find a teenager who doesn't carry an iPhone; most teens do not frequent Facebook.

You may have a purpose for making a TikTok video highlighting your budget proposal for the coming year, but the message should be catered to a young audience. TikTok is dominated by a younger audience. Facebook usually attracts older audiences. Know your audience and the platforms they are using to reach them. It is more time-consuming, but tailoring your message on each platform is more likely to hit the target audience and purpose.

Posts on the district's Instagram may look different than the posts issued on the superintendent's account. One way to frame it is like sharing a photo album. If you were asked to share your ten favorite pictures over the past year, there could be significant variability in what you select depending on the audience. What you share might look different for the Board of Education Chair than it does for your best friend. Posting operational information requires the same scrutiny.

One of the real benefits of social media is that posts are directed to your followers or subscribers. Those individuals are your dedicated audience and will automatically be availed of the information you share by virtue of the fact that they follow you. Still, when considering your audience, you must consider whom you want to target beyond your comfortable, supportive base.

Utilizing "tagging" or "mentions" of specific individuals in your post can inform those additional people. You may even target specific people, hoping your message is further amplified. In the training drill scenario, tagging the Mayor, Police Chief/Department, and Fire Chief/Department for them to repost your message could have amplified it to a viral level (at least locally).

Concerning operational social media messaging, this presents an opportunity to inform and acknowledge those who decide to finance your school projects and educate the community. A post about a roof replacement is hopefully not the most exciting message you share all year, but it may be one of the most important. Consider tagging the politicians who made funding for that project possible and thanking them for this vital upgrade to the facility in your post. This gives them an important update about the value of the investment and keeps them connected to the district. It also allows them to repost the information to reach more followers.

Engaging political figures through posts before the work is even proposed may help put the intended work on their radar before the proposal reaches them. If you know there is tremendous support for needed upgrades to a building, sending a post highlighting the work to be done while tagging the politicians who need to make that decision can be powerful. The post is even more valuable when they see the multitude of comments supporting the proposal.

Enlisting the support of others in operations efforts is more expansive than just political figures, however. For example, the Parent-Teacher Organization for a building may be an essential audience when planning building upgrades or responding to a facility issue. As previously mentioned, other town officials can also be your partners in amplifying messages. There is no rule against coordinating communications to reach the broadest audience or influence how the message is received. Inform those you are tagging or who share your interest that a message is forthcoming and request that they comment or repost. A well-placed call can mean the difference between 300 people reading a post and 3,000.

Putting It All Together

When I became Superintendent of the Cheshire Public Schools in 2016, our average district building was approximately seventy years old. The "newest" building opened at the same time Disney World did in 1971. In the fifty years since the last building was constructed, there have been numerous failed attempts to build new schools. A few buildings saw classroom additions, which did nothing to increase critical features such as kitchens, gyms, and libraries, but most buildings saw only obligatory maintenance to extend their lifespan. The most recent effort to propose new construction came in 2017.

The morale for school modernization hit a new low when the local fiscal authority refused to propose a new middle school to the voters. The silver lining in the otherwise dark cloud was that politicians were beginning to acknowledge that a position of limited maintenance was not a long-term solution. Yet, there wasn't enough broad community understanding and support for the substantial investment that new construction requires.

Convincing the broader community that it was time to invest in new schools was its hurdle to clear. Coordinating messaging around a successful school modernization plan would require a far-reaching and coordinated communications campaign. It was evident that there wasn't a clear understanding from the broader community about the need and the costs, not to mention the value of such a community improvement.

In the year following that failed attempt, the Town ultimately decided to create a committee to explore constructing new schools. What followed were years of discussions, evaluations, and proposals. The committee proposed the construction of two new large elementary schools (and closing three smaller schools) to alleviate a massive climb in primary enrollment and address the significant facility needs that existed at the primary level. The politicians understood the needs and the benefits of the vision the committee created.

With the Town's blessing, the voters would have a chance to weigh in through a referendum on Election Day in 2022. Of course, social media was present throughout the deliberations about which proposal to embrace. However, communicating with the community about the need and proposal would be critical in the months leading up to the referendum. Connecticut's rules around advocacy are clear in that no public money can be spent to advocate for a project sixty days before a referendum. That means it was only permissible to share facts, no opinions or requests for a yes vote, about the project once within sixty days of the referendum.

For example, a post featuring a classroom thermometer reading 90 degrees with students virtually melting in the background days before the referendum would be considered advocacy. This was true even if the post didn't technically cost money or mention the new schools. It was clear that we would be going to a referendum about 120 days before the vote, meaning we had about 60 days to share information advocating for the project and about 60 additional days to share logistical information such as the cost of the project or the date of the referendum.

All of the timing above, purpose, audience, and amplification strategies had to be played to perfection if we were to see the years of work come to fruition. There was one other tool we used to ensure that our time and resources had the most significant return possible. I had just heard about geofencing when I met with a marketing firm to identify strategies to educate our community on a pending school modernization project we were working through. Our community had not built a new school in fifty years, and educating the broader audience about the upcoming referendum would ensure a greater likelihood that they would at least be informed regardless of how people voted.

In short, geofencing is creating a virtual perimeter around a geographic area. Picture that you are drawing a line around a space on the map you want to target with your messaging. The space you can choose to geofence can be as small or as large as you wish. Given that we were seeking to communicate with town residents, our geofence was limited to the perimeter of the school district. The geofencing heightened awareness about the project, stimulated people to become educated, and ultimately became a key social media strategy that allowed us to educate our voters.

In geofencing, cell phone towers and Wi-Fi spots are utilized to identify cell phones within that area. When a cell phone enters the space, communication occurs between the cell phone and the tower, which shares information about the cell phone. Advertisers buy a specific demographic and send information to the phones that match that demographic profile. This explains why you might get advertisements for a restaurant close to your location or a special event like a concert that is occurring locally.

Cell phones within the geofenced area receive messages as part of a targeted advertising campaign. Messages are refined to reach a specific demographic through geotargeting. Understanding that the average American has more than seven social media accounts, using these platforms to educate your community was a powerful solution that we had never heard of, but had the potential to reach everyone who entered our community in a new way.

We engaged in a months-long geofencing strategy for an investment of a few thousand dollars. We targeted phones in the community owned by individuals of voting age. As those people scrolled through their feeds, they would see advertisements informing them about the new school proposal that directed them to our school modernization website. If these people didn't follow the news or have children in our schools, they might not have otherwise been aware of the issues behind the new school's proposal.

In the six weeks leading up to the referendum, we had 330,433 views! The town has approximately 30,000 residents. Using a

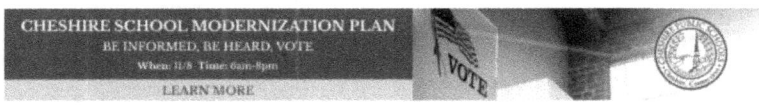

FIGURE 5.2. Cheshire modernization website. *Source:* Cheshire Public Schools.

conservative estimate that 20,000 residents were on social media during that time would mean that the average resident saw a school modernization advertisement more than sixteen times in six weeks. Throughout the campaign, we had nearly 700 people click from the advertisement to our school modernization website.

We were convinced that an informed voter was a voter who would vote in favor of school modernization despite a half-century of local voters failing to support such referenda. A local Political Action Committee was led by a very dedicated parent who took up the advocacy position when the sixty-day blackout window took effect. I also delivered many presentations to anyone who would listen, including one summer evening in a resident's backyard where only two people showed up prior to the blackout window.

As much as we felt that everything that could be done had been done, there was a lot of anxiety on the evening of the referendum. The vote was held on election day to ensure the best community turnout possible. As the results trickled in from each precinct, it

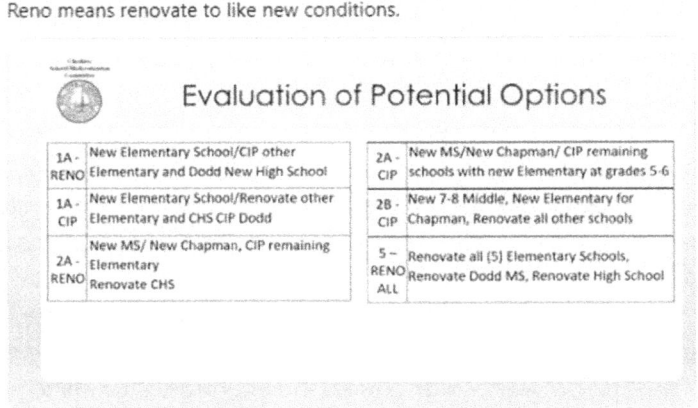

FIGURE 5.3. Cheshire modernization options. *Source:* Cheshire Public Schools.

FIGURE 5.4. Cheshire modernization committee meeting. *Source:* Cheshire Public Schools.

became evident that the hard work and efficient communication had paid off. The residents supported the referendum by a margin of 60 percent in favor to 40 percent opposed. While it may not look impressive, it felt like a landslide in our context.

Again, social media informed people about the project. The information gleaned through our communications gave them the capacity to advocate for the cause. Some naysayers would tell people that the project cost would double taxes. Those who were informed were able to share facts that countered that narrative. We would not be building new schools if we did not engage in social media to educate our stakeholders.

Another school district launched a well-orchestrated social media campaign to support building a new high school. Cost estimates of code-update rehabs, like new renovations and new construction, were shared. The message was simple: Can't make the official meetings? Visit us here for accurate and timely information. The number of followers demonstrated the community's interest in the project despite so few attendees at the actual meetings. Social media was the difference maker for us. Don't hesitate to utilize social media to advance your systems and operations efforts in your school district.

Social media can certainly get the word out to the public quickly. The district had just hired a new bus vendor in the middle of the school year. With current bus vendors struggling to find drivers and the marketplace becoming very competitive, the timing could not have been worse for this school district. Despite a thorough messaging campaign from the district, parents were not happy; in fact, they were becoming downright angry.

With many calls coming into the district's transportation office, another staff member was added to take calls from parents. While parents were no longer waiting for someone to pick up the phone, the answers to their questions did not make them feel better about the late bus situation. The district could do little about the lack of bus drivers, new drivers not knowing the routes, or buses running late every day.

Parents took to social media to express their concerns. Board of Education members took notice of all the complaints. Meetings between the administration and the bus company became more regular. Bus company executives even took questions from the Board of Education and parents. Everyone acknowledged the problem, but no one seemed to have a great solution. Allowing the problem to take on a life of its own on social media was not the answer.

The school system leaned into technology. With the bus company's support, the district launched an app that allowed parents to see where their child's bus is in real-time. They sent messages through parent communication with regular updates. Many of those messages made it to parents' personal social media networks. Every time the bus company hired a new driver, the community was informed. While busing continues to be a challenge, technological advancements and accurate social media posts have the district in a much better position.

Conclusions

As much as district leaders are focused on the power of social media to create a culture around learning, the benefits of social media in district operations can't be neglected. Political connections, facility improvements, human resources and recruiting, budget advocacy, and collaboration with other community organizations highlight some of the operational focal points your social media strategy can build around. The timing, purpose, audience, and platform considerations are leveraged to drive home messages and influence stakeholders to drive your school system forward.

That progress is grounded in educating stakeholders who can advocate and clarify on your behalf. That message was reinforced by an executive in the marketing firm. He said, "Social media is such a powerful way to connect with the community, but it works best when there is a clear plan in place." Whether it is an individual or marketing team, he stresses the value of active management of the account or accounts so that posts are "intentional, meaningful, and responsive." That focus sets the standard for your audience to know that your messages matter and focuses their attention when they see your post. As mentioned, posts have intentions. Focused messages turn those intentions into reality.

While reading the book's first chapter, you can begin by creating your why for social media. Chapter 2 shares how social media can assist with talent management and professional learning. Chapter 3 focuses on using social media to enhance educational curriculum and instruction. Chapter 4 centers on using social media to build positive school climates and cultures. Next up is Chapter 5, which discusses how to leverage social media for systems and operations enhancements. Now is our opportunity to tie it all together as we encourage educators to lead social media efforts and make connections in their schools.

As we began putting our fingers to the keyboard in preparing this manuscript, we have seen an explosion of social media users and numerous challenges created by school threats on social media channels. We have attempted to navigate these challenges safely and successfully. We have seen how one troubling social media post has frozen districts and communities. School closures, police searches, student expulsions, agency involvement, and community forums have impacted our schools and neighborhoods.

So what did we learn? How was our thinking influenced? Social media's power, reach, and impact is far and immensely powerful. We know that just as social media can spread fear, it can also be used to share current information and provide audience comfort and positivity. The start of this school year and the challenges social media posts have had on schools make us more determined to ensure that schools nationwide launch their personalized social media strategy.

School stakeholders are utilizing social media in many facets of their lives. Whether we agree with it or not, our students, staff, and parents receive information about their schools from social media posts. Schools must go social too and share accurate and timely information. Schools can also use the reach of social media to hire the talent they need to make a difference for their students. Teachers can use social media for personal and professional learning and growth. Many teacher platforms on social media share curriculum resources, instructional strategies, and assessment tools.

If there is one thing that educators have learned through their use of social media, it is that it's not the tool that matters most. What matters most is the reason for use and the audience it is designed to reach. Districts used to limit the number of people

FIGURE 6.1. Cheshire public school strings. *Source:* Cheshire Public Schools, June 6, 2025.

participating and the number of platforms used to share messages. Many districts posted participation caps on all messages, fearing dilution of the message. Given how people are informed by social media, it is entirely acceptable to have many people sharing the message through various social media vehicles.

While many worried about culpability and if too many posts would be seen as more spam, today's focus must be on the quality of the message, the credibility of the person posting, and the alignment with the district's vision and goals. Of course, the size of your district and the number of staff will influence your social media policy. Smaller districts may utilize teaching staff, coaches, and parent groups to support their social media campaign. Larger districts may require all social media posts to go through their communication teams.

Clarifying the district theme for your social media campaign will be necessary for all districts, regardless of size. Equally important will be determining who will be the gatekeeper and who is tasked and given the authority to post content about the district, schools, and students. Districts should also provide professional development

 **Cheshire Public Schools**
@CheshirePublic

Kindergartners at Doolittle School were using Lego pieces in clay to represent the two parts of an addition equation, then challenged partners to find the sum. #cheshirepublic #cheshirepublicschools #cheshirectpublicschools #doolittleelementaryschool

10:02 AM · May 23, 2025 · **88** Views

FIGURE 6.2. Cheshire public school instruction. *Source:* Cheshire Public Schools, May 23, 2025.

and coaching for all social media content creators, authorized users, and staff who oversee the social media campaign. If your staff needs to gain the technical capacity or expertise to leverage social media, consider partnering with an outside provider with the experience of utilizing social media successfully to improve organizational climate and culture.

Social media has also allowed schools to build and improve school climate and culture. Students and staff awards and ceremonies are easy to post and typically garner positive attention. Progressive schools are also using social media to gather support for school building projects, budget requests, and new facility constructions. As more and more schools recognize social media efforts, they must share their successes and lessons learned with other schools looking to positively impact their students, staff, schools, and community.

Further supporting the need to create a robust social media presence for public schools is evident in a Community Asks survey feedback graph. The survey allowed residents to share how they prefer to receive information from their municipality. While print newspapers, local news, text messages, the city website, and email were all viable options for residents, the overwhelming request for information was via social media. Seventy-nine percent of residents stated they prefer to receive information from their municipality via social media. Regardless of your thoughts on social media, these data are a clear reminder that social media must lead the way if we want to support parental involvement and engagement.

School and district leaders who want to connect with stakeholders should make sure that social media is one of their strategies. With clear data indicating that your citizens prefer to receive information via social media, the next question is what type of content they want from their municipality. Citizens are most interested in receiving information about programs and events, construction projects, public safety, and city-led initiatives. Social media may be the preferred way to receive information, but equally important is which information to share with stakeholders.

Social media's massive reach and loyal audience can provide school systems with a low-cost marketing campaign. Social media can improve the image of schools by simply sharing accurate

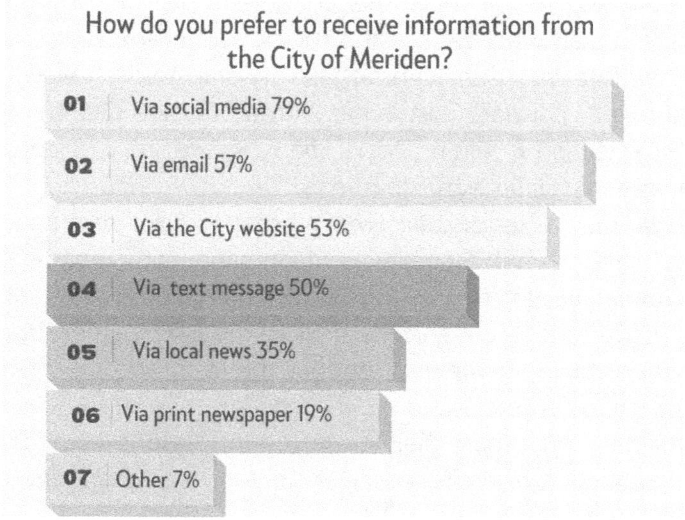

How do you prefer to receive information from the City of Meriden?

01	Via social media	79%
02	Via email	57%
03	Via the City website	53%
04	Via text message	50%
05	Via local news	35%
06	Via print newspaper	19%
07	Other	7%

FIGURE 6.3. How do you prefer to receive information from the City of Meriden? *Source:* Meriden Public Schools.

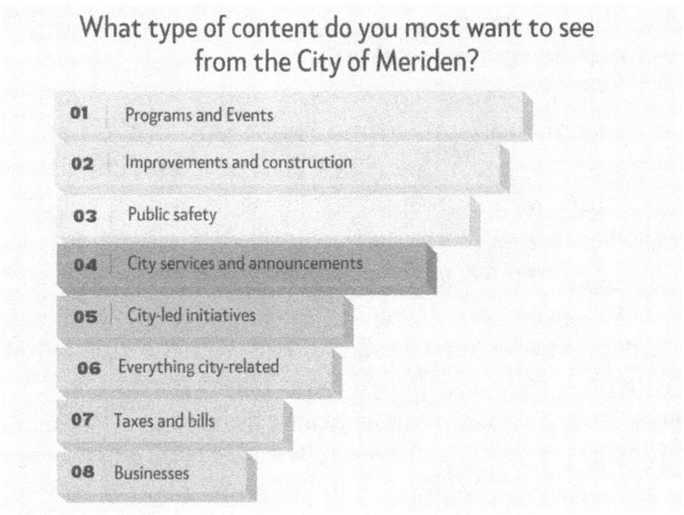

What type of content do you most want to see from the City of Meriden?

- **01** Programs and Events
- **02** Improvements and construction
- **03** Public safety
- **04** City services and announcements
- **05** City-led initiatives
- **06** Everything city-related
- **07** Taxes and bills
- **08** Businesses

FIGURE 6.4. What type of content do you most want to see from the City of Meriden? *Source:* Meriden Public Schools.

data. Improved graduation rates, standardized test scores, facility enhancements, community partnerships, and student and staff success stories offer the content to create an honest, open narrative with your stakeholders. Sharing positive stories on social media can and should include stories throughout the school organization, including food service, buildings and grounds, athletics, and the arts.

Students and teenagers remain prime social media users, as it has become how they communicate with others. Many students are encouraged to create social media content, learn essential skills, and increase their engagement and satisfaction with school learning tasks. Social media creation can help students

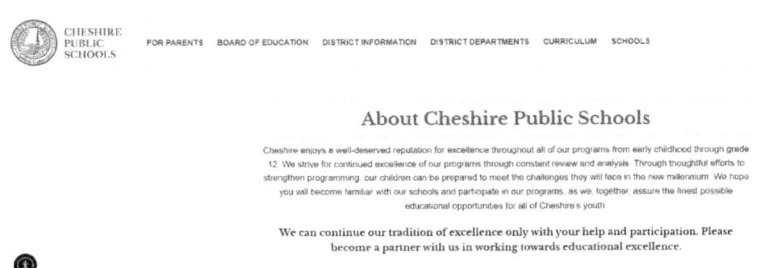

FIGURE 6.5. CPS website banner. *Source:* Cheshire Public Schools.

improve their marketing knowledge, writing ability, photography techniques, and communication skills.

While more and more schools use social media as a communication plan, too many schools and districts still need to create social media guidelines and policies. Schools should also inventory who is creating social media and contributing to their districts' social media campaigns. While district and school administrators remain vital participants and contributors, many districts' social media efforts include teachers, coaches, band and choral directors, and club advisors. Schools with the most ambitious social media campaigns have students playing a considerable role.

While individual social media platforms have certainly changed in popularity over time, social media is a vehicle for communication with students, staff, parents, and the community. Social media is an integral component of a school and district's world. Harnessing the advantages of social media will require schools to look at their

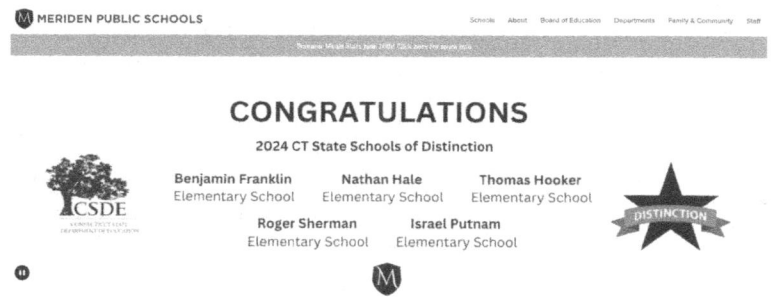

FIGURE 6.6. MPS website banner. *Source:* Meriden Public Schools.

FIGURE 6.7. Cheshire parent resources. *Source:* Cheshire Public Schools.

websites differently. Where do students, staff, and families go for information? Where can social media help build the district brand and garner attention? The school's website can and should provide all the documents a school consumer should need.

This is why it is so important that school districts see the importance of social media and that the district's website is utilized in tandem to inform and excite constituents. While the percentage of social media users continues to rise, ensuring that no one gets excluded can be addressed by an easily accessible, business-friendly, informative, and engaging website. We encourage schools to utilize social media as one component of their communication plan. Don't rely solely on social media or make it your exclusive social media platform.

Social media firms can support schools across the globe by addressing rogue social media accounts that prey on our students. Students should not be harassed, bullied, ridiculed, or misinformed by fake accounts claiming to be official school and district ones. Every moment false claims remain active, visible, and posted, targeted students are put at greater risk, and misinformation becomes the followers' new reality.

Many executive technology organization leaders have reached out to Facebook, Instagram, Snapchat, TikTok, Twitter, YouTube, and LinkedIn to express student safety concerns and the need for these social media giants to support schools and insist on verification requirements.

Here are ten lessons learned that can help all districts launch a successful social media campaign:

1. Stakeholders need to be taught. Teachers must be provided with embedded coaching, and students need to be taught online safety and digital safety skills. Provide our families with an easy-to-access help desk—launch training sessions for your resident seniors to learn from your high school students.
2. Learning environments need to be safe. Safety management software is vital, but remember the importance of personal relationships and trust.
3. Device user guidance needs to be clear. Guidelines provide parameters for students' use of devices in class and during the school day.

4. **Building administrators should use it.** Ensure building administrators post, tweet, and communicate with their stakeholders regularly.
5. **Common hashtags help.** A common hashtag builds connectedness and strengthens your district brand.
6. **Your web presence must be credible.** Official district and school websites can be expected to share accurate and necessary information. That is why we recommend embedding your social media feeds on your district and school websites.
7. **Options for notifications are needed.** Use notification tools and ensure that your messages are pushed to district and school media platforms.
8. **All district operations should be included.** Involve other key district departments in your social media plan. Food and Nutrition Services, Transportation, and Facilities have timely information to share with your community.
9. **A point person should oversee district social media.** Designate a point person for your communication outreach efforts or utilize private vendors to enhance your online presence.
10. **Good news needs to be shared often.** News coverage is quick to point out the challenges and struggles occurring in your community. Schools, thus, need to be the ones to share the great work of their students and staff, which we know is occurring every day in your schools across the nation.

Consider the areas for improvement in your district that a social media presence would best serve. Once you decide that it is a forum you will participate in, you need to be strategic in what you will use and how you will use it. You will want to have consistency in what and when you post. Once you decide to highlight teachers or students, you must ensure that all groups are represented equally. Once you begin posting to any social media site, stakeholders will be watching to see if their priorities are being represented. Are you promoting both elementary and secondary schools? Are all sports teams being highlighted? Are you recognizing academic as well as arts and music achievements?

Consistency is also essential in what messages you post and where you post them. If you establish a protocol that school delays will be posted to X, you have to ensure that each and every school delay is posted there. Your teachers, students, parents, and community stakeholders will come to rely on accessing the information on that platform. The first time you fail to post a school delay to X, you damage the trust relationship, and people are less likely to return to that location for important information in the future.

Remember your audience. Whom are you trying to reach? If you are putting a message out that you want students to see, is the social media platform you have chosen appropriate for students in that age group? Make sure you are not forcing students to use a platform that is not age-appropriate. Most social media platforms generate income through advertising, and you must consider the federal and state laws that govern advertising directed at children.

Parents as active school partners is a goal all schools aim to attain yearly. Check in with your parents to see what social media sites they use and inquire if the district is causing them social media overload. Also, learn from your parents what information they need and want from their schools. Is there a vehicle in place for parents to opt out of posts? What if parents do not want their child's name or photo in a social media post? How do parents express their views and desires?

Lastly, what if an unflattering perspective is used and posted through social media? Who determines whether or not it is used? In addition to these considerations, there are ethical considerations when launching a social media campaign. Schools must be aware of age restrictions and e-rate funding requirements. All of us are responsible for keeping our students safe, including being safe when they are online visiting social media.

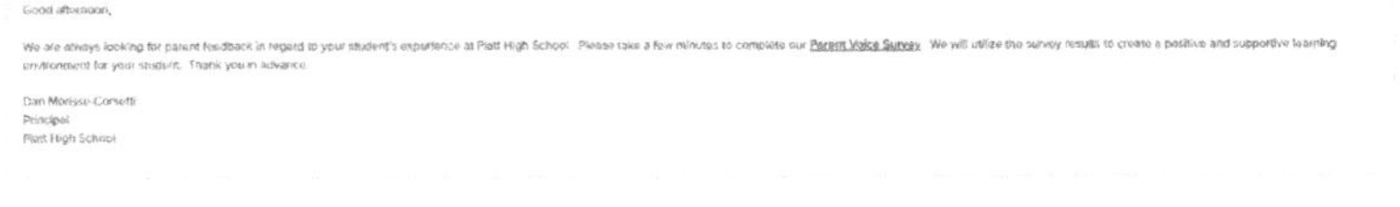
Orville H. Platt High School

2024/25 Parent Survey is OPEN

Daniel Corsetti • a month ago • Wednesday, Oct 16 at 5:00 PM • Orville H. Platt High School, PHS Board Members

Good afternoon,

We are always looking for parent feedback in regard to your student's experience at Platt High School. Please take a few minutes to complete our Parent Voice Survey. We will utilize the survey results to create a positive and supportive learning environment for your student. Thank you in advance.

Dan Morisse-Corsetti
Principal
Platt High School

FIGURE 6.8. Parent voice survey. *Source:* Daniel Corsetti, October 2024.

There are a lot of great materials and resources out there, but it is unlikely you will have a full-time social media team to make everyone happy. Focus on your district/school improvement priorities. Empower and trust your team to make posts that highlight the positive activities of your students and staff. Share a positive message, and remember to think before you post. Videos posted to YouTube and Facebook can provide valuable information in a timely, dependable manner.

Other districts have used social media to post interviews with staff members and students. These videos build credibility, so when something negative gets shared, there is no need to respond directly or definitively. While some individuals may use social media for negative reasons or to voice their complaints, school systems should model using it for informative, accurate, and helpful information. Tell your story, keep it real, and be positive always.

To rely on the benefits of social media platforms, we must teach students how to select videos of interest that would be helpful to them, not scroll mindlessly for hours. We should also teach students how to connect appropriately with others and create beneficial and educational videos. Students must track their usage, use their time effectively, and focus on their tasks. When students do this, social media becomes a learning tool, not a distraction.

Students should be encouraged to use social media to show and share their unique skills, talents, and abilities. They must know that college admission officials and future employers will see their social footprint. Students must also know that their posts have real consequences, such as school discipline, harming friendships and relationships, impacting employment, and alienating community members.

Don't use social media to respond to criticisms or attacks. Stay positive, stay factual, and remain intent on providing honest firsthand content. In this way, social media can allow community stakeholders to see the great work of the district up close and personally. Our advice to educational leaders is simple: if you are not using social media to communicate with your parents and community, START SMALL, and START TODAY!

The Art of a Hashtag

Using a shared hashtag across social media posts and platforms is a great way to build your district brand. As you are crafting your hashtag, consider the following:

- Does it make sense? Will people understand why this hashtag relates to your organization? Does it describe your core values and identify your brand?
- Does it have a different meaning to some people? In developing the #HereStudentsSucceed hashtag for the Meriden Public Schools, a communications company suggested using the #LivingtheDream hashtag. However, in the Meriden community, the phrase living the dream is a common sarcastic retort when asked, "How are you doing?" It denotes that things are not, in fact, going well.
- Does abbreviating the hashtag invoke a different meaning? Shortening #HereStudentsSucceed to #HSS doesn't pose a problem. However, shortening #AllStudentsSucceed is not the message the district wants to convey.

Now that you have experienced some of the challenges social media presents to school systems, it is time to create your own social media campaign for your school or district. Utilize the tips, strategies, and lessons learned to ensure that your social media campaign has a plan to go social, hire social, learn social, celebrate social, leverage social, and lead social. Your students, staff, and stakeholders will be users and consumers of social media content. Utilize social media content to share your story, set the record straight, and celebrate your successes.

As districts face declining budgets and staffing challenges, they can utilize social media to garner budget support and hire staff in hard-to-fill areas. As teachers and other district educators feel isolated and need more professional learning, encourage them to join professional networks on social media channels. When your district seeks approval for a new school building project, leverage social media to keep your stakeholders and supporters informed and engaged.

When your students and staff achieve great things in the classroom, on the athletic field, or on the main stage, use social media to acknowledge, applaud, and celebrate their efforts and successes. Lastly, we need honest, transparent leaders who use social media to lead passionately and persistently. We wish you the best on your social media journey; we will anxiously watch your story unfold on Facebook, Instagram, Snapchat, X, TikTok, LinkedIn, Pinterest, Reddit, YouTube, and more. Choose your platform and just get started! It is that easy.

In Closing

Social media is here to stay! Leverage social media and go social. Let social media help your school district improve and succeed by assisting with talent management and professional learning, enhancing curriculum and instruction, creating a positive climate and culture, supporting systems and operations, and leading with social media and making connections. Do not allow cell phone bans, the fear of AI, or social media mental health concerns to prevent you from launching a district social media campaign that is safe, educational, and supportive of district goals. Your students, staff, and parents will applaud your efforts.

Moving Forward

As the authors made clear throughout this book, social media is not only a ubiquitous aspect of students' lives; it permeates the lives and experiences of teachers, counselors, administrators, families, and other constituents. This aligns with findings from our *Social Media and Mental Health* research study. Although schools in our study banned personal device use in their buildings, students still felt the effects of what occurred on social media during the school day. One teacher shared,

> I can give you a scenario from today, like a kid didn't come to my class because of things that happen not in class [but] over social media and they were just in, like not a good mental health space because of all that drama that's happening over the social media space so they ended up staying and talking to another adult and not coming to class so, that student is really just not okay today from everything.

When discussing the prevalence of cyberbullying in a group chat for their children's non-school-affiliated sports team, a parent shared, "things said there definitely transfer outside of the team or outside of that, it doesn't stay online. What does that look like? How do you hold people accountable for things said that will affect other people?" As the authors noted time and time again, what occurs over social media and how that affects youth has an impact on school staff and administration. On a different end of the spectrum, other teachers agreed that students' use of apps such as Headspace, Calm, or "anything for meditation" has helped their students cope and transfer skills into the classroom. Further, many participants observed that celebrating students' accomplishments via social media positively affected their self-esteem. One counselor shared,

> We promote our students' successes, or highlight students who are doing well on our school social media platforms... it can build confidence in that student or students... so, using our adult versions of the platforms in a positive way for students to kind of emulate that is a way for kids to also feel good about themselves and see that adults notice them, are promoting them.

Social media and new technologies like AI will continue to emerge and be used by members of school communities, even if some community members wish they would disappear. We recognize that school district leaders are under immense pressure to restrict or ban students' access to social media, cell phones, and other personal technology. Yet, given the relevance of technology in the lives of students and other community members, the authors of this book offer a different approach for us to consider. Leaders can create a school culture where educators uphold reasonable parameters around personal device use while leveraging social media to foster student learning and success, enhance talent management and professional learning, and improve systems and operations. Fostering digital literacy and citizenship among all members of school communities, not just students, is vital to navigating a world where in-person and virtual boundaries are becoming blurrier each day.

Much of the public narrative on social media and technology use focuses on children. The scholarship on social media also focuses on this population. However, it is important to recognize that children's initial socialization to social media and technology occurs early in their lives before they ever step into a school classroom. This socialization continues throughout their youth, as they observe others, notably adults in their lives, using cell phones and other devices. Emerging research supports this. Nagata and colleagues (2024) found an association between parental screen use and higher problematic screen use among adolescents. They also identified that parents using screens as a reward or punishment to control behavior was associated with problematic game use and increased screen time. Participants in our study acknowledged this repeatedly. One parent created a digital media contract with their children where all parties agreed to certain phone and screen behaviors that they discussed and reflected on regularly. Other parents appreciated this suggestion and wanted more recommendations from other parents, schools, and community members to try at home.

Regarding role modeling, a counselor we interviewed noted,

> We have to think a little bit about how the adults are modeling their phone usage. You know, I've walked into classrooms and there's a teacher and a paraprofessional, and they're both on their phone while

they're [with] students, you know, working quietly at their desk[s]. You know, even in our own offices, you know my phone's right here. Obviously, when I'm engaged with the student, I'm not on it, but I don't think that's always the case. I mean adults are attached to their phone, just as much as kids are. It's by their side. So, you know, I've had students say that like, you all are hypocrites. Like, you are on your phones too. I see it right there on your desk. I walked by your office. I think, you know, that's talking about a whole cultural change as well and everyone being on board with them.

Our team has come to use an analogy related to smoking to describe how adults role model social media use for youth. Our current context is like telling children that smoking is bad for them but having teachers, parents, and other adults smoke in their faces. Regardless of the outcomes of social media use, if we hope to shift students' online behaviors, we need to address how adults role model the use of social media and other technology. As one high school teacher shared,

> I think educating students and parents is important, but similar to what we were saying about the cigarettes. We didn't know a lot back then and then as we started to learn about the dangers of smoking, now it's printed on packages. You can still choose to buy that pack of cigarettes. But we've educated you on the harmful effects.

It is likely that successful interventions to address these behaviors will need to be multifaceted and require a community-wide approach that extends beyond schools. In short, the onus to address students' social media and technology use must not solely rest on schools. Moving forward, we encourage school district leaders and other community members to collaborate not only to educate students but also to educate parents, educators, and others on the topics of digital literacy and citizenship, and role modeling.

Much of the scrutiny on student technology use focuses on personal devices. However, students often spend more time throughout the school day on school-provided laptops and devices (e.g., iPads), and children routinely receive access to these devices early in their school experiences. The scholarship on how school-provided technology devices affect students is limited and often dated. Yet, our research suggests that students regularly use these devices outside of their intended purposes. For example, one middle school teacher commented,

"They're very creative, they'll even say we're working together on a project and so they'll work on a Google slide presentation and they'll just communicate, like through Google [Slides]. So, they even will turn things into social media that were not meant to be used in that modality."

Moving forward, educators and scholars should pay more attention to how students use school-provided technology and examine and explore the associated outcomes.

We cannot predict exactly where technology is going. As demonstrated by the trends of the last decade and by the perspectives shared by this book's authors, it is moving faster than we can fathom. However, what we do know is that adolescence is a critical time for the development of positive well-being or mental health issues. Unfortunately, mental health issues among this population have reached a concerning high (World Health Organization, 2021). While not conclusive, it appears that technology may play a bidirectional role in this relationship (Weinstein & James, 2022). Therefore, it is essential that we proactively (1) provide sustainable and equitable mental health and educational resources for all students in schools; (2) invest in ongoing training, education, and development around digital citizenship, literacy, and agency for school staff, students, and families; (3) prioritize longitudinal research that investigates the bidirectional relationship of digital media use on well-being; (4) iteratively develop, refine, and implement research-informed school-based strategies that educate students on healthy digital media use and safeguards against its problematic use; and (5) embrace long-term research-practice partnerships between researchers, schools, families, and youth that contribute to this essential research and practice. As argued by the authors of this book, leveraging social media for the betterment of schools and students can be challenging. However, we hope this book introduces a refreshing, asset-based approach to embracing this challenge so that students thrive in a digital age.

Kathy C. Rohn
Assistant Research Professor
Department of Educational Leadership
University of Connecticut

Adam M. McCready
Assistant Professor-in-Residence
Department of Educational Leadership
University of Connecticut

References

Abrahamsson, S. (2024). *Smartphone bans, student outcomes and mental health* (Norwegian School of Economics, Department of Economics Research Paper Series). https://doi.org/10.2139/ssrn.4735240

American Psychological Association. (2023). *Health advisory on social media use in adolescence*. https://www.apa.org/topics/social-media-internet/health-advisory-adolescent-social-media-use.pdf

Anderson, M., Faverio, M., & Gottfried, J. (2023, December 11). Teens, social media and technology 2023. *Pew Research Center*. https://www.pewresearch.org/internet/2023/12/11/teens-social-media-and-technology-2023/

Moreno, M. A., & Radesky, J. (2023). Putting forward a new narrative for adolescent media: The American Academy of Pediatrics Center of Excellence on Social Media and Youth Mental Health. *Journal of Adolescent Health*, *73*(2), 227–229. https://doi.org/10.1016/j.jadohealth.2023.04.027

Nagata, J. M., Paul, A., Yen, F., Smith-Russack, Z., Shao, I. Y., Al-shoaibi, A. A. A., Ganson, K. T., Testa, A., Kiss, O., He, J., & Baker, F. C. (2024). Associations between media parenting practices and early adolescent screen use. *Pediatric Research*. Advance online publication. https://doi.org/10.1038/s41390-024-03243-y

Nesi, J., Telzer, E. H., & Prinstein, M. J. (2020). Adolescent development in the digital media context. *Psychological Inquiry*, *31*(3), 229–234. https://doi.org/10.1080/1047840X.2020.1820219

Nesi, J., Telzer, E. H., & Prinstein, M. J. (Eds.). (2022). *Handbook of adolescent digital media use and mental health*. Cambridge University Press.

Odgers, C. L., & Jensen, M. R. (2020). Annual research review: Adolescent mental health in the digital age: Facts, fears, and future directions. *Journal of Child Psychology and Psychiatry*, *61*(3), 336–348. https://doi.org/10.1111/jcpp.13190

Prothero, A., Langreo, L., & Klein, A. (2024, June 28). Which states ban or restrict cellphones in schools? *Education Week*. https://www.edweek.org/technology/which-states-ban-or-restrict-cellphones-in-schools/2024/06

Riehm, K. E., Feder, K. A., Tormohlen, K. N., Crum, R. M., Young, A. S., Green, K. M., Pacek, L. R., La Flair, L. N., & Mojtabai, R. (2019). Associations between time spent using social media and internalizing and externalizing problems among US youth. *JAMA Psychiatry*, *76*(12), 1266–1273. https://doi.org/10.1001/jamapsychiatry.2019.2325

Seabrook, E. M., Kern, M. L., & Rickard, N. S. (2016). Social networking sites, depression, and anxiety: A systematic review. *JMIR Mental Health*, *3*(4), e50. https://doi.org/10.2196/mental.5842

Twenge, J. M., Joiner, T. E., Rogers, M. L., & Martin, G. N. (2018). Increases in depressive symptoms, suicide-related outcomes, and suicide rates among U.S. adolescents after 2010 and links to increased new media screen time. *Clinical Psychological Science*, *6*(1), 3–17. https://doi.org/10.1177/2167702617723376

Weinstein, E., & James, C. (2022). School-based initiatives promoting digital citizenship and healthy digital media use. In J. Nesi, E. H. Telzer, & M. J. Prinstein (Eds.), *Handbook of adolescent digital media use and mental health* (1st ed., pp. 365–388). Cambridge University Press. https://doi.org/10.1017/9781108976237.020

World Health Organization (2021, November 17). Mental health of adolescents. https://www.who.int/news-room/fact-sheets/detail/adolescent-mental-health

About the Authors

Mark D. Benigni, EdD, is the award-winning superintendent of the Meriden Public Schools, the school system from which he graduated and where his children attended. Dr. Benigni is recognized as a transformative leader, guiding his district to its highest achievement scores through collaboration and innovation. During his over fifteen years at the helm of the Meriden Public Schools, he has led the district to two National Blue Ribbon Schools, numerous state Schools of Distinction, and many district awards.

Barbara A. Haeffner, the assistant superintendent for teaching and innovation, is known for leading digital transformation and creating student-centered learning environments where student voice and choice truly matter.

Susan O. Moore, director of Instructional Technology and Curriculum for the Meriden Public Schools, leads the district's initiatives to ensure equitable access to digital resources and leverages technology to improve student outcomes. In 2023, she was honored as the National Chief Technology Officer of the Year by the Consortium of School Networking (CoSN).

Jeffrey F. Solan, EdD, has served as the superintendent of the Cheshire Public Schools since 2016. In that time, Cheshire has realized the highest academic achievement in the district's history and engaged in the construction of two new schools. He has recently fostered a relationship with the Gyeongsangnam-do Office of Education (GOE) in the Republic of Korea, serving as a keynote speaker for their Future of Education Conference in Changwon in 2023. Cheshire has subsequently hosted several teachers from GOE in exchange programs through their schools.